REDISCOVERIN

D1262309

THE CELTS

REDISCOVERING THE CELTS

The True Witness from Western Shores

MARTIN ROBINSON

Fount
An Imprint of HarperCollins*Publishers*

Fount is an Imprint of
HarperCollins*Religious*
part of HarperCollins*Publishers*
77–85 Fulham Palace Road, London W6 8JB
www.christian-publishing.com

First published in Great Britain in 2000 by Fount

1 3 5 7 9 10 8 6 4 2

Copyright © 2000 Martin Robinson

Martin Robinson asserts the moral right to be
identified as the author of this work

A catalogue record for this book is
available from the British Library

ISBN 0 00 628153 2

Printed and bound in Great Britain by
Caledonian International Book Manufacturing Ltd, Glasgow

CONDITIONS OF SALE
This book is sold subject to the condition that it
shall not, by way of trade or otherwise, be lent, re-sold,
hired out or otherwise circulated without the publisher's
prior consent in any form of binding or cover other
than that in which it is published and without a
similar condition including this condition being
imposed on the subsequent purchaser.

All rights reserved. No part of this publication may be
reproduced, stored in a retrieval system, or transmitted,
in any form or by any means, electronic, mechanical,
photocopying, recording or otherwise, without the prior
permission of the publishers.

This book is dedicated to my wife Lynda
for whom the Celtic tradition has
come to mean so much.

CONTENTS

PREFACE

 Rediscovering the Celts has been a long time in the writing. An awareness of the reality of an ancient Celtic spirituality probably began for this author at the age of ten following a visit to the Isle of Iona together with a group of American pilgrims. In those times the boats stopped at the Isle of Staffa and, in truth, the dramatic geography of that island probably made more impression on a ten-year-old than the rather flat and uninteresting landscape of Iona. But a question remained. What was it about Iona that brought a group of Americans thousands of miles to visit and wonder?

Interest in the Celtic saints was rekindled during the 1970s as part of many family holidays to the west of Wales. As with Cornwall, the place names of Wales quietly echo a remarkable spiritual history. Holiday villages such as Llangranog (the church of St Cranog), contain churches with their own parish histories, lovingly collected and published by local historians. Picking up such brochures, attempting to visit the remote caves of the saints and wondering how and why these distant figures had exercised deep converting power and authority led to a long lingering interest in the mission of the Celtic saints.

Even so, as many existing authors never tire of asking: There have been so many books written about the Celtic church in recent years – why write another? Two different but related streams have inspired this volume. First, there is an awareness that the Celtic church is exercising a curious and widespread interest both within but also beyond the Christian community. As Peter Millar, Iona Abbey's Warden has recently expressed it: '... you'd be amazed at the number of people who get off that ferry and say: "I feel, at last, I am at home." What on earth do they mean? Many of them aren't even Scottish! You see people actually hugging the stones.'[1]

The sense of coming home is an important theme in the midst of a culture that is revealing symptoms of fragmentation and where extreme individualism seems to triumph over meaningful community. The theme of Celtic spirituality seems to be striking a resonant chord with many in both church and culture.

Second, there is a growing realisation that the Celts were not just a minor presence who disappeared after Whitby. The Celtic saints represent a major element in the reconversion of Europe to the Christian faith. One Irish American author has amusingly picked up this thread in the rather journalistic title of his book *How the Irish Saved Civilization*.[2] This is not just a good title; it is also substantially true in the sense that the Celtic monasteries were significantly responsible for preserving the light of an older civilisation throughout that period known as the Dark Ages.

---

[1] Paul Vallely, *Independent*, 30 May 1998, p. 28.
[2] Thomas Cahill, *How the Irish Saved Civilization: The Untold Story of Ireland's Heroic Role from the Fall of Rome to the Rise of Medieval Europe* (Doubleday, 1997).

The growing realisation that the Celts have a place of importance in the history of western Europe, acting as a hinge of history, as one author has expressed it, is not just the outcome of a growing Celtic cottage industry. A renewal of interest requires information to sustain it. To some extent, much of the revised thinking concerning the Celtic church has occurred because, for nearly a century, scholars, particularly in Ireland, have been patiently gathering enough information to make a re-evaluation possible.

A broader shift in a scholarly understanding of the role of the Celts in the development of the Western church has been noticeable. It is instructive to compare a representative of an older scholarship, for example Margaret Deanesly, in her book *A History of the Medieval Church*, first published in 1925, with a contemporary scholar such as Peter Brown and his book *The Rise of Western Christendom*, first published in 1996. While it could be argued that Deanesly's work does not cover exactly the same dates as Brown's, there is sufficient overlap to have allowed for a similar coverage of the Celts to have taken place. As it is, whereas Brown devotes chapters to the Celts, Deanesly dismisses them in a few paragraphs.

This gradual growth in scholarly understanding, has allowed a significant re-evaluation of the role of the Celts to take place. But the work of scholars has not been confined to Ireland and the British Isles. Continental scholars have become increasingly aware of the role of the Celtic missionaries in evangelising parts of Europe from the major river valleys of western Europe to obscure valleys in Switzerland through to eastern Europe.

While visiting my former professor at his home in Switzerland, he pointed across the lake in front of his home to a particular mountain. 'On that mountain lies the cave of the

Celtic saint who first evangelised this area,' he told me. The name of that saint could be found in a number of nearby place names.

One element of this revisiting of the Celts has often been stimulated by an interest in ancient cultural life. But the major focus of this book is not so much cultural curiosity, fascinating as that can be, as a burden for mission. The Celtic saints were nothing if they were not missionaries. That was their passion.

Many have remarked that the reality of a post-Christian West includes much that is neopagan in its thinking. The growing awareness that the West represents a particularly challenging mission field is bound to cause us to ask whether we might learn some lessons from those who conducted the task so successfully many centuries ago. The encounter with paganism in the past might shed some light on the effort to dialogue with the neopaganism of today.

Such a concern also carries with it some acute dangers. It is all too easy to opt for a cosy romanticism or to want to read into the past whatever we might want to find. The later chapters of this book address these dangers very directly.

A further difficulty arises from the technical issues surrounding the level of writing. For the most part books on the Celts tend to fall into two very clear categories. One category is scholarly, detailed and occasionally obscure. The second category could be described as the popular and romantic. I have attempted to write a book that bridges these categories. The intent is to be both accessible and rigorous and this is not an easy combination. The reader must judge to what extent the pages that follow have succeeded in their intent.

In writing this book I have been greatly helped by the work of my researcher, Joseph Gelfer, who has undertaken valuable work in locating resources, helping to evaluate the major

themes and assisting in much of the footnoting. His patient
assistance has been much appreciated by the author.

The Celtic tradition holds a special place for the apostle
John. The gospel of John paints a vivid picture of the last
supper as a place of great intimacy. Around the table, John is
portrayed as leaning on the heart of Jesus. This image speaks
deeply of the spiritual tradition represented by the Celts –
passionate, intimate, valuing friendship. John's gospel comes
to us as a work of intellectual insight and intimate passion.
This unusual combination suggests something of the contribution of the Celts to mission.

1

UNCOVERING THE CELTS

It is almost impossible to live for any significant period of time in a Celtic country and be unaware of the feeling that those who are English are somehow foreign. The first language of the majority may well be English but feelings of identity, race and cultural assumptions all point to a gulf not easily bridged by such notions as Britishness. Such feelings can easily feed nationalism though they do not inevitably take such a political turn. As recently as the 1960s nationalists in Scotland often felt like a rather fanatical and even sinister breed, deliberately brooding on ancient hates rather than looking with confidence to the future. These ancient suspicions found more tangible expression in sentiments surrounding sports fixtures rather than parliaments.

But moods and times change and the closing decades of the twentieth century have witnessed a rise of interest in all things Celtic. As the twentieth century closes and a new century begins a concern for Celtic cultural expression is much more mainstream than it has been for some centuries. This Celtic resurgence has ranged across a wide range of cultural, linguistic, political and religious themes.

The extent of this revival of a sense of Celtic identity is all the more remarkable when contrasted with the situation at the beginning of the twentieth century.[1] At that time, the various Celtic languages were in severe retreat. Cornish was reported as being entirely dead. Gaelic in its Scottish form was to be found only in parts of the sparsely populated Highlands and Islands. Welsh was spoken more widely but was still in retreat. Children in Welsh schools were strongly discouraged from speaking the language in public. It was thought of as a language for the home and not suitable for public conversation. Gaelic in its Irish form was encouraged by the new government in the Republic of Ireland but had a great deal of ground to recover if it was ever to compete with English, while Breton was also discouraged by the French authorities. Even as recently as the 1960s it would have been unthinkable to imagine that schools in Wales would teach all subjects in Welsh and that the children of English 'incomers' would be required to learn Welsh in order to participate in education.[2]

---

[1] Perhaps the only popular cultural reference to the Celts at this time was Alexander Carmichael's *Carmina Gadelica*. However, even this collection of prayers and blessings really had little to do with the Celtic tradition actually rooted in history, rather it was a reflection of contemporary rural workers and their expression of faith which happen to be geographically located in 'Celtic' territories.

[2] The extent of Welsh medium education has grown considerably in recent years. At present, just over a third of the primary schools in Wales teach at least part of the curriculum through the medium of Welsh, and Welsh is used as the medium of instruction for at least six subjects in 46 Welsh secondary schools. The Education Reform Act 1988 established a new status of definition for Welsh medium schools and for the teaching of Welsh as a second language. Schools teaching at least five or more subjects through the medium of Welsh were classed as Welsh medium schools, and Welsh Second Language was introduced as a Foundation subject into all schools in Wales (from Research into Welsh Medium Education and the Teaching of Welsh by the National Foundation for Educational Research at www.nfer.ac.uk).

Today, virtually all of the Celtic tongues are staging a gradual recovery. Television stations produce a good amount of their output in Welsh in Wales, and Gaelic in Scotland.[3] Road signs in Wales are bilingual with the Welsh language taking precedence. It is a requirement for those in public service to speak Welsh. Cornish seems to have avoided the absolute extinction that was threatened and has seen a modest growth in the number of those who know the language.

The changed position of Celtic languages has been mirrored by a recovery in cultural activities. Celtic festivals such as the Welsh eisteddfod and the various Celtic festivals in Brittany have become hugely successful. These occasions for the celebration of poetry, music, dance and a wide variety of folk traditions have not only acted as showcases for the best in Celtic culture but have stimulated further participation, pride and interest in Celtic causes. The Breton festivals, in particular, have encouraged a sense of a wider Celtic identity which transcends the purely national and linguistic traditions identified with the nations of Scotland, Ireland and Wales. In large part this is because the Bretons have been so active in inviting the participation of significant numbers of Celtic performers from other lands. To some extent this has been a deliberate attempt to counter the weight of pressure on Bretons to be part of a wider French culture.

---

[3] BBC Scotland produces 125 hours of Gaelic programmes every year. BBC Radio Scotland has a special frequency for Gaelic programming which transmits a full 45 hours per week in Gaelic. In Wales BBC Cymru produces 520 hours of Welsh programmes every year and 18 hours each day on the radio. S4C produce a further 20 per week of Welsh programming. Even BBC Northern Ireland has 18.5 hours of Gaelic programming on television per year and 4.5 hours of radio each week.

Cultural movements on this scale inevitably contain a political dimension.[4] In the case of Ireland, the cultural revival has flowed strongly from the new political reality created by the struggle for and then the fact of Irish independence. In Scotland and Wales, and to a lesser extent in Brittany, the growth of Celtic consciousness has helped to feed demands for greater autonomy for these regions or nations.

But it would be wrong to think that the interest in all things Celtic is solely a matter of the reawakening of the identity or national consciousness of those parts of the British Isles (and France) that used to be referred to rather disparagingly as 'the Celtic fringe'. Interest in the broader Celtic culture and past of Britain as a whole extends beyond the more obviously Celtic parts of Britain, and indeed beyond the matter of language and culture. Many who are firmly part of Anglo-Saxon English life have become aware that an older Celtic culture preceded the arrival of the English and are anxious to become better acquainted with that older tradition.

The religious dimension exercises a particular fascination for many who wish to uncover a Celtic past. This applies both to those who are attempting to recover a pre-Christian Celtic religious tradition[5] and to those for whom the Celtic Christian

[4] See Oliver MacDonaugh (ed.), *Irish Culture and Nationalism: 1750–1950* (Macmillan, 1988); John Hutchinson, *The Dynamics of Cultural Nationalism* (Allen & Unwin, 1987); Terrence Brown, *Ireland: A Social and Cultural History 1922–1979* (Collins, 1981).

[5] For simple, yet accurate, accounts of the pre-Christian Celts, readers might refer to Miranda Green, *The Gods of the Celts* (Alan Salton, 1986) and Nora Chadwick, *The Celts* (Penguin, 1971).

tradition is a source of real interest and inspiration.[6] It is hard
to say just how many are involved in some kind of quest for the
recovery of Celtic religious traditions, but the shelves of book-
shops suggest that interest in both the pagan and Christian
Celtic traditions is significant and growing.

What then is happening to produce this wide range of
interest? Can we detect some broader movements which would
help to explain this resurgence of curiosity in matters Celtic?
Three themes at least are contained within this Celtic revival.
First, the re-emergence of nationalism as a potent cultural and
political force across Europe and beyond has made its presence
felt in the latter years of the twentieth century. In some cases,
such as in Bosnia, the forces of nationalism have thrown a
malignant shadow across whole communities and even over
surrounding nations.

Nationalism is not always frightening, threatening or mur-
derous though the passions aroused are always pregnant with
such possibilities. The dramatic changes in Eastern Europe flow-
ing from the collapse of the former Soviet Union has allowed
nascent nationalism to emerge as a potent theme throughout
Eastern Europe and Central Asia. In a different way, the
creation of large, but more flexible political unions such as
the European Union, has given fresh impetus to the hopes of
conquered cultural minorities. A broader European framework
has created a practical possibility for a viable future without
reliance on the nation state within which national minorities
have been reluctantly bound, sometimes for many centuries,

---

[6] There are numerous communities around the United Kingdom and Ireland
who attempt to preserve the spirit of the early Celtic Christians within a
basic community rule. Such communities can be found on Iona, Lindisfarne
and in many other locations.

without ever being fully absorbed. Nationalist sentiment is certainly one element in the renaissance of Celtic culture.

A second factor is the widespread reappearance of a kind of popular romanticism within Western culture more generally. For many the future now looks more frightening than exciting. The world represented by the politics of hope, epitomised by the presidency of John F. Kennedy, lies in ruins. A deep scepticism concerning the present, the future and the immediate past has caused some at least to look to a much more distant past as a time when the world seemed to be more understandable, stable and romantic. In our imagination, at least, past cultures had no difficulties with gender roles or social cohesion. In past societies people had fewer rights but owed such strong responsibilities to one another that rights actually seemed more secure. A more sober investigation soon reveals that life in past generations could be grim indeed, but that does not stop some people from wanting to bring elements of the past into the present and to reinterpret them in contemporary guise. A strongly romantic theme runs through much recent popular culture, for example in the films *Rob Roy* and *Braveheart*. Music which purports to have Celtic roots has emerged within the youth pop culture,[7] while Celtic art and handicrafts have formed the basic sales ingredient of hundreds of cultural centres and gift shops throughout Ireland, Wales and Scotland.

A third contributory stream can be located in the emergence of a new interest in spirituality, especially of a mystical

---

[7] The biggest bands to fit into this category must be U2 and Simple Minds. There are, though, a plethora of Celtic roots band touring the UK music scene. Moreover, many bands who are not obviously 'Celtic' in roots employ various dimensions of music which has derived from Celtic lands.

variety, within the West. The Celts in general are often credited with particular qualities of mystical appeal. The legends associated with Arthur and Merlin have helped this perception, but more generally, the idea of druids who have a secret and hard-won knowledge has an obvious attraction for a generation which has surveyed the spiritual landscape and found it barren indeed.

For those with an interest in the Christian dimension of Celtic spirituality, there is a much richer vein waiting to be tapped. The pagan Celtic past is hard to reconstruct as there is little available in written records. Much more is available, however, in written form and in accessible archaeological remains, to bear testimony to the Christian contribution of the Celts. The very place names of the Celtic hinterlands bear eloquent witness to the work of hundreds, if not thousands of Celtic missionaries and saints. The thousands of churches which are dedicated to such saints preserve stories concerning these remarkable Celtic holy men and women.

It is not difficult to see how romanticism, nationalism and mysticism can combine in differing degrees to produce a profound nostalgia and interest in the Celtic period of British history. All three of these themes are themselves part of a wider reaction currently impacting Western culture. The cracks now appearing in the dominant modernity of the last few centuries, imbued as it is with a naïve belief in the inevitability and benefits of progress and its handmaiden, technology, have allowed religious and romantic themes to re-emerge. The tendency of modernity was always to create larger and larger states with their accompanying institutions. Such states have tended to become focused on a single dominant culture to the detriment of weaker or minority cultural or national groups within that same state. The reaction of postmodernity has encouraged the renewal of the culture of minority groups and fostered their hopes for at least a limited degree of national expression.

Some of these reactions carry within them huge potential dangers. The line between an interest in folk culture and the power of the *volk* with its implication of a desire for racial purity is sometimes all too thin. But the interest in Celtic themes is not all about reaction, it is also legitimately concerned with discovery. Over the last one hundred years, scholars have been patiently and carefully reconstructing a legitimate history of the Celts as a people and a culture.[8] While there are no complete answers and there are most certainly significant differences of opinion on a range of key issues, a number of clear elements can be reliably documented.

WHO ARE THE CELTS?[9]

We can say with some certainty that by approximately 1,000 BC the Celtic peoples migrated from east of the Danube into central and western Europe. This migration saw settlements in those lands which we now know as Austria, Germany, Switzerland, France, Spain, northern Italy (around the Po valley), the area of ancient Turkey known as Galatia, and

---

[8] The waters have been muddied over the past five years or so in this process with the use of a revisionist reading of history. The revisionist project will, eventually, bring wonderful new light to the world of history, yet at the moment it has the dangerous effect of rendering void the many scholastic tomes upon which the study of the Celts have been based.

[9] This section owes much to Myles Dillon, and Nora Chadwick, *The Celtic Realms* (Weidenfeld & Nicolson, 1967). Any reader would do well to consult them for more in-depth information about the roots of the Celtic peoples.

throughout the British Isles. The settlement in these lands saw the emergence of the cultural identity known as La Tene which thrived (especially in artistic terms) until the Roman conquests and, in the case of Ireland and Pictish Scotland, beyond the period of Roman expansion.

They were known to the Greeks as the Keltoi (from which the modern term 'Celts' is derived) or the Galatai (from which the area of ancient Turkey known as Galatia is drawn). The Romans called them the Galli or Gauls. Both the Greek and the Roman terms really mean 'barbarians'. From the perspective of the Romans and the Greeks, these barbarians were the dominant social, military, political and cultural force to the north of their territories. The term gives a particular insight into the apostle Paul's occasional references to barbarians as if they represented a separate category alongside Jews and Greeks.[10]

Although it is accurate to think of the Celts in terms of a common culture and a broadly similar language, it is not the case that they formed a unified political entity. Rather, even in specific areas such as Gaul or Ireland, the Celts were organised as a series of tribes that were able to work together on the basis of a loose confederation depending on the strength of local and regional chiefs and on the nature of the enemy that they faced. In certain areas, notably in Spain, the incoming Celts merged with the local population (in the case of Spain, the Celtiberi) to form a related but distinct grouping. The disparate nature of these tribal groupings meant that the various Celtic tribes were often at war with each other. Occasionally

---

[10] Acts 28:4; Rom. 1:14; 1 Cor. 14:11; Col. 3:11. Sometimes Paul does not use the actual word *barbaroi*, but words rendering the meaning of 'foreigner' or 'non-Greek', See Gerhard Kittel, *Theological Dictionary of the New Testament* (Eerdmans, 1965), I, pp. 551–2.

they were able to mount effective alliances with each other. One of these alliances resulted in a significant defeat of the Romans around the year 450 BC. During this campaign Rome itself was laid to siege. But despite this victory, the inability of the Celts to form long-term alliances with each other meant that eventually the Romans were able to isolate, conquer and subdue most of the Celtic peoples over a period of time. The various Roman accounts of the Celts reveal a degree of apprehension concerning what they felt to be their barbaric appearance. The Roman historian Diodorus writes:

> Their aspect is terrifying ... They are very tall in stature, with rippling muscles under clear white skin. Their hair is blond, but not naturally so: they bleach it, to this day, artificially, washing it in lime and combing it back from their foreheads. They look like wood-demons, their hair thick and shaggy like a horse's mane. Some of them are clean-shaven, but others – especially those of high rank, shave their cheeks but leave a moustache that covers the whole mouth and, when they eat and drink, acts like a sieve, trapping particles of food ... The way they dress is astonishing: they wear brightly coloured and embroidered shirts, with trousers called bracae and cloaks fastened at the shoulder with a brooch, heavy in winter, light in summer. These cloaks are striped or chequered in design, with the separate checks close together and in various colours.
>
> [The Celts] wear bronze helmets with figures picked out on them, even horns, which made them look even taller than they already are ... while others cover themselves with breast-armour made out of chains. But most content themselves with the weapons

that nature gave them: they go naked into battle ...
Weird discordant horns were sounded, [they shouted in
chorus with their] deep and harsh voices, they beat
their swords rhythmically against their shields.[11]

The Celtic migrations to the British Isles took place in at least
two major waves. The first wave came in the very early years of
the Celtic expansion through western Europe. These peoples
were identified by language as the Goidelic-speaking peoples
which gave rise to the closely related forms of Gaelic spoken
in Ireland, the Isle of Man and later in Scotland. The peoples
who came in a second later migration were identified by a
different language form, the Brythonic-speaking peoples. Their
migration gave rise to the dominant forms of language spoken
in southern Britain (surviving as Cornish), Wales, and later
in Brittany.

Inevitably this rather general picture was complicated by
smaller movements and migrations. Three examples illustrate
these later processes. First, some Irish expansion occurred in
the western regions of Wales resulting in the establishment of
some small colonies there. The local inhabitants called these
people *gwyddel* which meant 'savages' from which comes the
term 'goidel' and hence the Goidelic tongue.

Second, changes in the original five divisions of Ireland
took place between the years AD 300 and 400. The original
five divisions of Ireland became dominated by two major ruling families which pushed the original people of Ulster into a
small coastal kingdom known as Dal Riata. Eventually even
this small kingdom was absorbed by the northern Ui Neill clan

---

[11] Oldfather (trans.) *Diodorus of Sicily* (William Heinemann, 1967), III, 5.

and from this base further expansion took place across the Irish sea in south-western Scotland. The kingdom of Dalraida was established in present-day Argyll. These people were known as the Scotti by the Romans and eventually gave their name to the whole of present-day Scotland.

Third, partly as a result of the invasions of the Anglo-Saxons, there came a large migration of Celts from Southern Britain in the latter half of the fifth century, especially from Cornwall, to the Celtic lands in what is now called Brittany (under Roman rule known as Armorica). It is likely that the original Celtic population of Brittany was not large and these people were overwhelmed by the hostile arrival of the Britons. The language now spoken in Brittany owes its origins to this much later invasion of southern Britons and not to the earlier Celtic population. In the same way the term 'Brittany' derives from the later invasion of Britons and not from the original Celtic population.

This complex mosaic of a broadly Celtic culture across large parts of northern Europe was further complicated by the expansion of the Roman Empire. From a Roman perspective, the two dominant Celtic groupings were those of the Gauls and the Britons. The conquest of Gaul and its subsequent absorption into the Roman Empire really brought to an end the existence of a clear, separate Celtic life and culture. In the British Isles, the position was much more complex. Eventually, the whole of southern Britain (present-day England and Wales) together with southern Scotland, was brought under Roman rule. Northern Scotland and Ireland were never conquered by the Romans.

The Romano-Celtic culture that prevailed for much of the first four centuries of the Christian era was clearly part of the empire, but some elements of Celtic culture, particularly language, survived, so that following the withdrawal of Roman authority, a recognisably Celtic influence was still identifiable, especially by comparison with the invading Anglo-Saxons. The island of Ireland remained entirely Celtic in culture and this influence re-established itself in Scotland after the Roman withdrawal and had some influence in those parts of Wales where colonies were established. The broad contours produced by Roman influence were important in the gradual conversion of the various Celtic peoples to Christianity.

2

THE COMING OF CHRISTIANITY

 The specifically Celtic nature of many of the areas of the Roman Empire was not as important for the spread of Christianity as was the fact of the empire itself. Only later, as the empire collapsed and Celtic culture re-emerged did the Celtic nature of these areas assume a real importance.

GAUL

The incorporation of the province of Gaul into the Roman Empire meant that to a large extent the story of the coming of Christianity to Gaul was an integral part of the growth of Christianity in the empire as a whole. A number of centres were important, notably, Poitiers, Tours and Lyons. In each of these cases, leaders from other parts of the Roman Empire were crucial figures. For example, Irenaeus (AD 130–202) was Bishop of Lyons in the latter part of the second century. He was originally from Smyrna where it is said that he witnessed the martyrdom of Polycarp. Irenaeus' main concern was to combat Gnostic tendencies in the church as a whole. His horizons were therefore towards Rome and further east, much more than towards a Celtic mission. In fact, large numbers of people whose ancestors had been part of a broader Celtic culture did become part of the church in these and other Christian centres, but that is not the same thing as the creation of a Celtic church in the formerly Celtic Gaul.

SOUTHERN BRITAIN

It cannot be said with any degree of certainty when Christianity first came to the British Isles. Most scholars speculate that individual Christians must have come to Britain amongst the Roman legions as sailors, merchants and Roman officials. Most sources note the presence of bishops from the British church at the Council of Arles in 314 and Rimini in 359. We do not know how widely Christianity had spread or was practised prior to Constantine's edicts which gave Christianity an entirely different standing throughout the empire. However, we do know of at least the martyrdom of St Alban, St Julius and St Aaron.

Following the Constantinian period, St Gildas suggests that the British accepted Christianity, but without much enthusiasm.[1] It is hard to say with what degree of accuracy Gildas spoke, but we do know that once the Anglo-Saxon invasions began, significant numbers of priests were put to

---

[1] Gildas is an odd figure often compared to St Jerome due to his sympathies for the Romans. While often seen as an important Celtic saint, Gildas held many Celtic kings responsible for the breakdown of British society. He was concerned with order and high morality which he found most in a Roman model of church and state. Gildas' *peregrinatio*, which took him to Brittany, must therefore be seen just as much as an alienation from the clergy and kings of Wales as a typical Celtic wandering. For Gildas, see Elissa Henken, *Traditions of the Welsh Saints* (D.S. Brewer, 1987), ch. 11.

death and churches sacked and burnt. Persecution helped to shape the self-understanding of the British church. British Christians were strongly identified with the Celtic language and culture which re-emerged in Britain following the Roman retreat. The British church suffered along with the general population and hence was strongly identified with what it meant to be British and a Celt. The pressure and persecution that came with the arrival of pagan Anglo-Saxons meant that the church in southern Britain came to be confined to the Celtic hinterland in south-western Britain and Wales. So great was this persecution that there is no single recorded instance of a Welsh or Cornish Celtic missionary working amongst the Saxons.

When St Augustine arrived as part of the Roman mission to England, he knew of the existence of a British church but contact was difficult and from Augustine's perspective, unrewarding. The well-documented meeting of Augustine with representatives of the Celtic church proved to be entirely unfruitful.[2] There was no meeting of minds, hearts or vision. But the problem at this stage was not so much a conflict between a Roman church and a supposed Celtic church as the cultural and ethnic tension that existed between a missionary to a conquering people, the Saxons, and an already indigenous church amongst a persecuted people. In the period between

---

[2] Such as Bede, A History of the English Church and People (Penguin, 1988), II, 2, where Augustine attempted to bring some of the British bishops into Catholic unity around certain issues such as the calculation of the date of Easter. Bede tells us that 'despite protracted discussions, neither the prayers nor the advice nor the censures of Augustine and his companions could obtain the compliance of the Britons, who stubbornly preferred their own customs to those in universal use among Christian Churches' (ibid.).

the departure of the Romans and the arrival of the Saxons, the importance of the church in Southern Britain did not lie in any attempt at mission amongst the Saxon pagans of England as amongst the Celtic pagans of Ireland.

IRELAND

Without question, the conversion of Ireland is associated overwhelmingly with St Patrick.[3] But this does not mean that there was no Christian activity before his arrival. As with Roman Britain we have no way of knowing exactly how Christianity first came to Ireland or when or with what strength. The probability is that Christianity spread in Ireland as it did in other places; traders brought the new faith, Irish travellers abroad were converted, some of those who were captured and brought back to Ireland to serve as slaves may even have brought the new faith into the homes of their new masters. Although we can only speculate about origins, we can say with more conviction that Christianity did exist in Ireland before the coming of Patrick, not least because the writings of Patrick indicate that this was so. In addition to Patrick's testimony, we know from Prosper of Aquitaine that Pope St Celestine sent to the Scots (the Irish) 'who believed in Christ', their first bishop, Palladius, whom he had ordained, in 431.

However, the work of Palladius and indeed the progress of the Christian faith before his arrival was considerably overshadowed by the undoubtedly enormous contribution of St Patrick to the conversion of Ireland. The story of Patrick is

---

[3] One popular and easily available book about Patrick is Alannah Hopkin, *The Living Legend of St Patrick* (Grafton Books, 1989).

well known even though the original sources are limited. He was born in the last quarter of the fourth century, the grandson of the priest Potitus and the son of a deacon, Calpurnius, in the area of Banavem Taberniae. There is some difficulty in knowing the actual location of this place since usage of the place name ceased. There are a number of schools of thought as to where Patrick's birthplace should be located. The two most prominent suggest that it was either in Glamorganshire, near the mouth of the Severn or that it is associated with Dumbarton near the mouth of the Clyde. All we can say with certainty is that Patrick was a Briton who was seized by Irish pirates when he was aged sixteen and that he was taken as a slave to Ireland.

His task as a slave was to tend sheep and during this period his rather nominal Christian faith took on a new significance. After six years he managed to escape and found a ship some two hundred miles away from his place of captivity, which took him across the sea. Patrick does not tell us accurately whether he landed on the continent or on mainland Britain. We know, however, that during this time he endured a short period of further captivity before eventually finding his way back to his family.

Upon his return, the conviction grew that he was called to return to Ireland as a missionary. In order to prepare for this task, Patrick travelled to Gaul. Some suggest that Patrick went to the islands of Lerins off the coast of Provence and others say that he studied at Tours. Whichever is the case, once prepared, Patrick did return to Ireland, probably in the year 432. He took with him a number of companions and centred his mission in the part of Ireland we know today as Ulster. Although we do not have a detailed account of the progress of his mission, it seems likely that a key ingredient surrounds his encounter with the pagan king at Tara, the centre of political power and pagan worship in Ulster.

The subsequent conversion of the king heralded a rapid progress of the Christian mission in Ireland so that together with the other Christian missionary work that was taking place, Ireland relatively quickly became a predominantly Christian centre largely as a consequence of a broadly Romano-Celtic and Gallic missionary enterprise. This development was to have an enormous significance for a Europe which was about to undergo cataclysmic change as a consequence of vast new migrations of largely pagan peoples entering western Europe from central Europe and beyond.

SCOTLAND

The general spread of the Christian faith throughout the Romanised parts of Britain would have caused the faith to be present in some parts of southern Scotland. To this generalised presence was added a specific missionary enterprise undertaken by St Ninian. We know that St Ninian, a native of Cumbria received his teaching in Rome and travelled throughout Gaul settling eventually in Galloway. It is almost certain that he spent some time with St Martin at Tours and without question dedicated his work to St Martin, modelling his centre, known as Candida Casa ('the white house') on the monastery at Tours.

St Ninian worked at the end of the fourth century amongst the Picts. It is a matter of debate as to how far his work extended or even as to whether it endured. Some of Patrick's later comments can be taken to mean that the Picts of southern Scotland later apostatised and that therefore the later work of St Columba was decisive in the conversion of the whole of Scotland. This was certainly Bede's perspective. Some scholars take the view that St Ninian's work was much more important in the spread of Christianity and therefore that St Columba's work simply added to the earlier foundation of St Ninian. A few scholars take the view that St Ninian ought to be thought of as the founding father for Christianity in Scotland, not to the extent that Patrick was in Ireland or even as David was in Wales, but possibly more like Aidan in the later Ionian mission to England.

Whatever the role of St Ninian in Scotland as a whole, there is no doubting that the work at Candida Casa spread beyond Galloway. Parts of the north of England were impacted. It is also true that visitors came from Ireland and probably from parts of Wales to benefit from the monastic community established by St Ninian.

By the year AD 450, we have a picture of a British Isles in which Christianity played a significant role. The links with an earlier Romano-British civilisation were evident. It was Celtic in the sense that there was an indigenous Celtic culture which had either survived beyond the Roman retreat or had never been ruled by Rome at all. But it was not an isolated and distinct Celtic church. Rather, the links with the continent were strong. Missionaries had come who had not been Celts at all. Some Celtic missionaries had received training on the continent, such as in the case of St Ninian. Certainly, there was no separate Celtic liturgy or tradition that could be recognised as something distinct from the generality of regional churches that had spread throughout western Europe. There was clearly a strong bond of contact between the emerging Christian centres along the west coast of Scotland, parts of England, Wales and Ireland, made possible by the ease of travel across the Irish sea, but that degree of contact did not by itself give rise to a single distinct, Celtic form of faith that was identifiably different from Christianity found elsewhere.

But what we see up until this time, is only the potential for a distinctively different Celtic form of the faith, not its actualisation. The factors that gave rise to a uniquely Celtic expression of Christianity need to be discussed in more detail in the next chapter. For the moment we only need to note that the period 450 to 600 was marked by an astonishing movement amongst the Celtic peoples which led to the deep conversion of the Celtic nations and laid the foundations for a flowering of what we now can call Celtic Christianity.

CONVERTING THE CELTS

How did this process of conversion take place? A more strongly monastic expression of the faith emerged simultaneously in a relatively few centres in Wales and in Galloway in southern Scotland (at Candida Casa). From these centres we see a pattern of development which flowed from Wales (particularly the south and the south-west) to Cornwall, Brittany and Ireland. A lesser, but still important, influence flowed from Candida Casa to Wales and more particularly to Ireland. From this initial impetus, the flowering of monastic forms of Celtic Christianity, learned from the Welsh and to some extent from the Scots, matured in Ireland and then returned to Wales, Cornwall, Brittany and Scotland. This work amongst the Celts then overflowed to England and to continental Europe. By tracing the interconnectedness between some of the important centres and their founding saints we can illustrate the progression of a distinctively Celtic Christianity.[4]

---

[4] A somewhat exhaustive account of the interconnectedness of Celtic communities can be found in E. Bowen, *Saints, Seaways and Settlements* (University of Wales Press, 1977). This book also goes towards expelling the myth that Celtic communities and saints lived in wild and remote places all the time by reminding us that a hop from Iona to Ireland for these communities was no more difficult than a trip today from Iona to London by car.

Wales

Some of the earliest saints founded monasteries near their place of birth. St Cadoc, for example, at the height of his career in the opening decades of the sixth century, established his monastery at Nant Carfan, west of Cardiff near his birthplace of Newport.

Other saints active in Wales had also arrived as missionaries. These included St Illtud (450–535) who, according to the life of Samson,[5] was from Armorica and had come to Britain as a warrior to fight the Saxons. Illtud went on to found his own, much famed, monastery at Llantwit Major which continued in building a network of influence and learning. Following his time at Llantwit Major, St Samson went on to engage in mission in Cornwall and Brittany, where he is recognised as one of the founders of the Breton church.

Perhaps more famously, Illtud was to influence St David (462–547), who was one of his students. David worked for a time in Cornwall before establishing his own important centre in Pembrokeshire. It was from the centre known as St David's in Pembrokeshire that he established his reputation as the founding father of Welsh Christianity.

The network expands with St Gildas (c. 500–570), another student of St Illtud. It is thought that Gildas came from Clydeside in Scotland, and after studying with St Illtud spent time in Ireland before later living in Brittany. Thus the Welsh saints were inextricably bound with the establishment of Celtic Christianity, not only in their own land, but also beyond.

---

[5] There are two versions of Samson's life to draw upon: the early seventh-century Latin *Vita Samsonis* and the twelfth-century *Vita in Liber Landavenis*.

Ireland[6]

St Finnian of Clonard in Meath is thought to have been the shaper of Irish monasticism following the time of Patrick. He was deeply influenced by both St Cadoc and St Gildas, having spent time in Wales. His monastery followed a strict monastic rule partly derived from St David's in Wales. Clonard was famous for the hundreds of missionaries trained there, amongst whose number can even be counted Columba and Columbanus. Another famous saint to spend time at Clonard was St Brendan who himself went on to establish a significant monastery at Clonfert in Galway around the year 650, and was held as one of the twelve apostles of Ireland.

St Kevin, a slightly later but important Irish saint, founded a monastery at Glendalough in Wicklow.

A second St Finnian, a contemporary and friend of St Brendan, was trained at the later Candida Casa (see glossary), the influential monastery at Withorn founded by Ninian. Finnian went on to found the single most important monastery in Ireland, in terms of scholarship, at Moville near Belfast. It was here that St Columba was trained.

A further key centre was that of Bangor in Ulster, founded in 558 by St Comgall. The key thread here is that Comgall was trained by St Finnian at Moville. In turn, Bangor trained many hundreds of missionaries, the most important being St Columbanus. Bangor was reputed to have had four thousand monks living there at one time.

---

[6] An excellent and detailed history of Irish saints and their spirituality can be found in D. O'Dwyer *Towards a History of Irish Spirituality* (The Columba Press, 1995).

Scotland[7]

As we have seen, St Columba spent time at Moville.
According to legend his period at Moville resulted in serious
controversy. He allegedly made a copy of one of Finnian's most
precious books without permission. In the Ireland of those
times this was a serious offence and the resultant trial gave
rise to an intense armed conflict between the supporters of
Columba and those of the high king who put him on trial.
Following this rather disgraceful start to his monastic life,
Columba travelled to Scotland with twelve companions and
settled on Iona.[8] The land was given to him by the local ruler,
Conall, who was a distant cousin of Columba. The island had
been used as a centre for religious devotion long before the
coming of Christianity and had been consecrated for Christian
use either by St Ninian or one of the earlier Irish missionaries
such as Finbarr who had preceded Columba.

As noted in the previous chapter, the present-day Argyll
was then an Irish kingdom known as Dalraida. But the position at the time of Columba's arrival was complex. In Roman

---

[7] See W.A. Hanna, *Celtic Migration* (Pretina Press, 1985) for an interesting
anthropological account of the migration of the Celts into Scotland.

[8] A romantic reading of Columba's departure from Ireland is becoming less
popular. A later medieval life of St Molaisse has it that Columba consulted
Molaisse as a confessor and was advised to go into perpetual exile from
Ireland to expiate the sins of having caused so many men to die in battle. It
is also suggested that the pilgrimage was imposed on him by the Synod of
Teltown to which Adamnan refers in his biography of Columba. The date of
the synod lies between the battle and Columba's leaving Ireland. One may also
sensibly consider that after the battle and the Synod of Teltown, Columba was
merely weary and chose to leave Ireland in the hope of releasing his religious
commitment from the entanglement of Irish dynastic politics.

times, virtually the whole of Scotland had been the territory of
the Picts. There is some debate as to whether or not the Picts
were a branch of the Celts separated in time and so in language, or whether they were a people who preceded the Celts.
Still others see them as a mixture of Celts and pre-Celtic
people. No-one can be certain, whatever their view. What we
can say is that the Picts were divided by the Roman invasion
into those southern Picts who were influenced by Roman life
and the northern Picts who were never conquered by the
Romans. The arrival of the Irish with their kingdom of
Dalraida further complicated the picture with regard to the
southern Picts. Further, in the period following the year 500,
the Northumbrian Angles were pressing the borders of the
southern Scots to a considerable degree.

To this position was added the further complication of a
renewal of hostilities from the northern Picts. King Brude,
whose seat of power was based in Inverness, had invaded the
kingdom of Dalraida in 560 and defeated the Irish. This ostensibly Christian base was therefore significantly undermined by
its military defeat at the hands of a consciously pagan king. It
is therefore not difficult to imagine that the earlier gains of
St Ninian had been undermined by the incursion of pagan
Angles from the south, defeat by those from the north and
possibly an absence of dynamic and cohesive leadership elsewhere. More than one-and-a-half centuries separate Columba
and Ninian and, apart from the activities of a few Irish missionaries in Argyll and Galloway, we hear of no other significant leaders in this period. At the very least, the work of St
Ninian was in need of renewal and clearly, in relation to the
north of Scotland, in need of extension.

From Iona a gradual missionising took place along the
western seaboard leading eventually to a colonisation of the

Hebrides, the Orkneys and even of Iceland and the Shetlands. But Columba could not afford to ignore for long the dominant influence of King Brude. Approximately two years after his arrival in Iona, Columba and his party set out on a mission to take the gospel to Brude and his people.

Columba's biographers give a great deal of attention both to the journey and to the event. Rightly so. The encounter was not just with one who was a power in the land but also with the powers behind that power. The accounts make great play of the role of Brude's foster father, Broichan, who was apparently a druid. This is significant, not just in relation to the influence that Broichan had over Brude, but it stands as a broader symbol for the confrontation between Christianity and the older pagan beliefs. The standing stones, so important in the pattern of pagan worship, gradually received Christian inscriptions. The Celtic cross, as well as other Christian symbols were carved on many important standing stones, centres of the former pagan religious system. Clearly these inscriptions were not random acts of Christian vandalism so much as the outcome of a power encounter.

The account given by Adamnan in his life of Columba, records the journey to Inverness in order to see Brude. The journey itself was full of miraculous incident as was the departure. According to the story, the opposition from the druids was so great that Brude could not be won to Christ. Columba and his band of followers had to leave the stronghold of Brude without success. But it was on the homeward journey that the druids, and in particular Broichan, overreached themselves. The druids conjured up a storm as Columba was about to set out, but Columba called on the assistance of Christ and 'no sooner was this order executed, while the whole crowd was looking on, than the vessel ran against the wind with extraordinary speed. And after a short time, the wind, which hitherto had been against them, veered round to help them on their voyage.'[9]

The winning of Brude to the faith signalled the spread of Christianity throughout Scotland, even in those parts where Brude held no sway. Iona trained and sent many who established centres elsewhere. But here the similarity with Irish monasticism ends. Unlike Ireland where each monastery and every abbot owed allegiance to none but themselves, the new centres in Scotland felt their relationship with Iona very keenly. Columba, though only a priest and not a bishop, in fact acted as a missionary primate for the whole of Scotland. The influence of Iona built on the earlier work of Ninian but did so in a manner that cemented the place of Christianity in the hearts, minds, social, political and cultural life of Scotland.

It is not an exaggeration to suggest that the work of Columba was actually formative in terms of the emergence of nationhood itself. Two illustrations make the point. First, Columba was instrumental in persuading the Ulster Dalraidans to give up their power of tribute over their Scottish colony. In this sense he was the original advocate of home rule for that part of Scotland which was under foreign domination. Second, Columba was asked to crown the new King of Dalraida after the death of Conall. Some suggest that the new king sat even then on the Stone of Scone. The association of this act with the gradual emergence of the kings of Dalraida as a key influence in the development of Scotland as a nation helped to integrate Christianity and nationhood in a way that arose from

---

[9] Adamnan, *Life of Saint Columba*, trans. William Reeves (Llanerch Enterprises, 1988), XXXV, p. 94.

a grass-roots popular piety, rather than as an imposed foreign faith.[10]

The conversion of the Celtic peoples created the missionary base from which a wider missionary movement could develop. But the process of conversion had not just produced a logistical basis for expansion; it had also created an authentic form of spirituality well suited to the conversion of the new pagans who now dominated large parts of Europe.

---

[10] A revisionist reading of history, such as Sharpe's would suggest that at this time there is no way of knowing what the majority of the population in this 'age of sins' thought about such religious enthusiasm and it is possible that at the time of Columba's death many of the Irish people and most of the inhabitants of Scotland were still pagan. To those involved in the monastic movement, however, it was something of tremendous importance. We must remember that these are the people who left the historical record of the time and it is through their eyes that it must be viewed. St Ciaran of Clonmacnoise and St Uinniau, mentioned several times in the biography of St Columba, also founded communities. Columba did not, therefore, belong to the first generation of saintly monastic founders.

3

A MISSIONARY FORCE

A CELTIC CHURCH

As we have seen in the previous chapter, by the year 450 Christianity occupied an important place in the life of the peoples of the British Isles. The various Anglo-Saxon tribes had begun to arrive in England by that time but were not yet a dominant presence. We could therefore say that the term 'Celtic Church' really meant the church as it existed amongst the predominately Celtic peoples of the British Isles. However, between the years 450 and 600 there came a significant flowering of Christianity amongst the Celts of Ireland. This 'golden age' of Christianity, expressed as it was in both fervour and learning produced a distinctly Celtic expression of Christianity which was more than just a description of the geographic location of Christian faith. Various Celtic distinctives played an important part in this western form of church which was carried by means of a vast missionary enterprise to other parts of central and western Europe. This missionary expansion coincided with the arrival of the then pagan Anglo-Saxons

in most parts of England and more widely in western
Europe.[1]

What was it that caused both fervour and learning to develop so dramatically? A number of writers suggest that the single
most important hallmark of this Irish and Celtic Christianity
centred on the introduction and development of a particular
kind of monastic life. According to this theory, the Irish church
prior to the coming of Patrick was organised on the normal
diocesan model. The coming of Patrick and the subsequent
completion of the task of converting the Irish continued the
same model. But following the death of Patrick, there came a
remarkable shift in this historical pattern. Monasteries prolifer-
ated to such an extent that these centres of learning and spiritual zeal came to dominate the Christian landscape.[2] Bishops were
often part of the monastery and in most cases bishops were subject to the leaders of the monastic communities – the abbots.[3]

---

[1] From the end of Roman occupation to the mid-fifth century the Saxons
had only been raiding the British shoreline. Traditionally it has been
Vortigern, who in c. AD 425 became the high king of southern Britain, who
betrayed Britain to the Saxons after a series of bad judgements and fierce battles in the second half of the fifth century. A full account of this process can
be found in the opening chapters of Peter Berresford Ellis, *Celt and Saxon:
The Struggle for Britain* (Constable, 1993).

[2] For an accurate up-to-date account see L. Bitel, *Isle of the Saints* (Cornell
University Press, 1990), or for a quicker account see Philip Sheldrake, *Living
Between Worlds* (DLT, 1995), and Martin Reith, *Celtic Spirituality* (Iona pam-
phlet, 1991). An interesting account of monasticism with special reference
to education and scholasticism can be found in K. Hughes, *Church and
Society in Ireland AD 400–1200* (Variorum Reprints, 1987).

[3] It must be remembered that the status of bishop during this period of
Celtic Christianity was not as grand as it is today. There were many bishops
during this time as we can tell when we hear that Columba took twelve
bishops with him to Iona.

The spread of Christianity by Celtic missionaries became syn-onymous with the spread of monastic centres. Each of these centres acted both as the place that trained leaders and as the centre that sent out missions to the surrounding countryside. It was often the role of bishops to lead the missions that the monasteries oversaw. (A later chapter will deal in more detail with the nature of monastic life.)

The argument that follows from this core contention concerning the centrality and importance of the monastery suggests that four other factors served to power monastic development into missionary endeavour. First, in recent years, there has come a fuller recognition of the impact of the sheer numbers of missionaries which emanated from the Celtic homelands. Although it is true that some individuals became especially well known, it is also true that their work was complemented by the labours of thousands of others, some of whom give their names to hundreds of churches in places such as Brittany, Wales and Cornwall, others of whom laboured and died with no record of their achievements. Careful research has produced a more detailed knowledge of where some of these individuals lived and worked. Bede tells us that the monastery of Bangor-is-Coed, located on the Dee, near Chester, comprised some seven cloistral divisions each of which contained at least three hundred monks. In more recent times we have gained an awareness that many individuals who trained there went out and ministered; they did not simply stay near Chester.[4]

Second, although it has long been known that the style of the Celtic monastic foundations was different in a number

---

[4] Louis Gougaud, *Christianity in Celtic Lands* (Four Courts Press, 1992), p. 60.

of important respects from that of the Benedictine model which was to predominate later, the significance of that difference has only recently been debated. Most scholars suggest that the inspiration for the Celtic model came from the eastern Mediterranean, probably through Martin of Tours.[5] But though the Celtic model was inspired from further east, it was not identical to eastern models either. Some unique Celtic ingredients were fused with a tradition that owed much to the saints of the North African desert. Many of these ingredients in the Celtic monastic style will be described in more detail in later chapters.

Third, the period of time encompassed by the Celtic missions had been unappreciated until recently. The myths surrounding the encounter at the Synod of Whitby sometimes created the impression that the Celtic missionary period began with Patrick and faded shortly after Whitby. While it is certainly true in an English context that the thirty-year period immediately prior to Whitby represented a remarkably energetic flowering of missionary activity, it is also true that a clearly Celtic (sometimes identified as an Irish) mission lasted until well into the tenth century. Indeed some traces of Irish monastic life on the continent of Europe continued until much later. The abbeys of Nuremberg and Vienna ceased to be exclusively Irish in 1418 when they passed to the Benedictines, and St James at Würzburg was taken over by German monks as late as 1506.[6]

---

[5] See Christopher Donaldson, *Martin of Tours: The Shaping of Celtic Spirituality* (Routledge, 1980).

[6] Gougaud, *Christianity in Celtic Lands*, p. 184.

Fourth, the theme of exile or *peregrinatio* is especially identified with the Celtic saints. The extent and missionary significance of these journeys is now better understood. Their travels
for Christ took them throughout the Low Countries, France,
along the Rhine valley, into Switzerland, Austria and northern
Italy. Some Celtic saints were thought to have laboured as far
afield as Russia and amongst other Slavic peoples. The journey
for Christ was not just an aimless wandering; it was a journey
with mission in mind. It was an exile from home and hearth
but, except in some exceptional cases, it was not an exile from
the company of others, still less from the church itself. The
purpose of the journey was to preach the gospel in such a way
that a local church would come into being. The special nature
of the *peregrinatio* will be discussed in a later chapter.

CELTS AND THE CONVERSION
OF THE ENGLISH

Columba died in 597 and in the same year, possibly within
days, St Augustine landed on the Isle of Thanet, sent directly
by Pope Gregory to work with the English.[7] The work of
Augustine initially proceeded quickly. He had originally come
with the knowledge that Bertha, the wife of King Ethelbert
of Kent, was a Christian. The church of St Martin's in
Canterbury had been reopened prior to Augustine's arrival.
The conversion of Ethelbert resulted in a significant number
of converts amongst his subjects.

Not only was progress in Kent rapid, but kings nearby who
owed allegiance to Ethelbert began to receive missionaries.

---

[7] Bede, *A History of the English Church and People* (Penguin, 1988), I, 25.

In 604 the King of the East Saxons, Sigibert, converted. His seat of power was London and he built the first St Paul's. Raedwald, King of the East Angles, converted and although none of his people followed his example it represented an encouraging new foothold. This progress, together with the establishment of a diocese based on Rochester, represented a hopeful start toward Gregory's ultimate goal of a system of twelve dioceses with two archbishoprics. Admittedly, Gregory's hope had been for one archbishopric in York and one in London. Why these two centres when neither reflected the pattern of Saxon power? Clearly, the former Roman imperial pattern of power was in Gregory's mind when he instructed Augustine and, in fact, the ultimate outcome was not so very different from just such a pattern.

But this early progress turned out to be short-lived. Ethelbert died in 616 and his son who acceded to the throne was a pagan. The whole missionary enterprise was under threat. The bishops of London and Rochester, Mellitus and Justus, had to flee the country and the Archbishop of Canterbury, Laurentius, was on the verge of doing so before conditions eased. Ethelbert's son Eadbald came to accept Christianity, ostensibly through the work of Laurentius, and so Kent at least was secure for the faith. However, it was forty years before the East Saxons returned to the faith and another bishop could be consecrated. In the meantime, Mellitus succeeded Laurentius at Canterbury.

Although Christianity was now well established in Kent the earlier momentum towards the conversion of all the English peoples had been lost. Despite these setbacks, the work in Kent had succeeded in making some unexpected progress in the north of England. In 625 Ethelberg, the Christian daughter of Ethelbert married King Edwin of Northumberland. Edwin had become King of Northumbria by defeating the then king, Aethelfrith, in 616. He had earlier deposed the family of Edwin who had fled to the court of Raedwald. Ethelberg took Paulinus with her as chaplain. Before Paulinus went north, he was consecrated as a bishop by Justus, who had succeeded Mellitus as Archbishop of Canterbury. Paulinus had been one of the small group whom Pope Gregory had sent as extra workers to assist Augustine in 601. Edwin was gradually won to the new faith.

The drama that accompanied his conversion included the famous incident when Edwin called a council of advisors which included political and pagan religious leaders. During the council one noble told the story in which he compared human life to the flight of a sparrow which flew into a lighted hall from the winter darkness. During its short flight through the warm hall it experienced a brief moment of light and warmth before entering the winter darkness again. The suggestion was that Christianity might offer hope of light in the darkness of the afterlife. After accepting the faith, Edwin was baptised in a wooden church built in York for the occasion. Paulinus became the bishop of York but his work was halted in 632 or 633 by the unexpected death of Edwin killed in battle by the Welsh king, Cadwallon, and his pagan allies from the Saxon kingdom of Mercia under Penda. Paulinus was forced to flee to Canterbury and with his departure the Christian advances in Northumbria were quickly reversed.

Events in Northumbria now took a rather different turn. In the power vacuum that followed the death of Edwin, Eanfrith, one of the sons of Aethelfrith, attempted to take the throne. He in turn was killed by Osric, a king of Deira. A year after this event, another son of Aethelfrith, Oswald, became king. Oswald, together with his brothers and sisters had earlier fled to Dalraida where he had been baptised and had learned to speak Irish fluently. The relatives of the former king, Edwin, were now in Canterbury and so Oswald, wishing to introduce his subjects once more to Christianity, turned to the influence of Iona for help.

The abbot of Iona at this time was a monk by the name of Segene. He had known Oswald during Oswald's exile on Iona and responded to his appeal for help by sending a monk named Colman. This choice appears to have been unfortunate since Colman returned after a short while with the report that the people were not receptive to his message. Bede recounts the story of Colman's return and records that Aidan pointed out that Colman's approach might have been too severe. He suggested that the people might have needed milk before being offered meat. His kind concern led his brothers to think that Aidan might be a better choice than Colman. Segene did not give up and sent Aidan to take up the work again. Aidan settled near the royal court of Bamburgh on the island known to us today as Lindisfarne.

Aidan proved to be both patient and wise. Following the Celtic monastic tradition, he chose twelve followers. Two of these were from Oswald's own family, his half-sister Aebbe and his daughter Elfleda. Both of these had been brought up in Iona and so spoke Irish fluently. These were undoubtedly very helpful to Aidan who did not at first speak Saxon. One other of those chosen by Aidan was Hilda, later to become the Abbess of Whitby. She had been baptised by Paulinus during his earlier mission and so it is possible to imagine that not all of those won for Christianity in the earlier period had been permanently lost to the faith.

According to Bede, the work of the community at Lindisfarne was supplemented by the coming of many other

Irish missionaries. We do not know if Bede was referring to the Irish of Dalraida in Scotland or to monks from Ireland itself. Indeed both places probably supplied helpers as news of the open opportunity in Northumbria spread. What is more certain is that the place of Christianity in the north of England became safe and secure. It was certainly assisted by the continued patronage of the royal family but it is clear that Christianity's roots went deeper than conformity to a royal whim. It was from this secure base in the north that the work of evangelisation proceeded to other parts of England.

From this point on there is a good deal of debate amongst historians as to the relative importance of the wider Celtic missionary effort as compared with that of the Roman missionaries based initially in Kent. No-one disputes that Northumbria was clearly brought to Christianity through the work of the Celtic missions or that Christianity in Kent owed its origins to the work of Roman missions, but the significance of other developments is disputed. There is little dispute concerning the main facts, but the interpretation of the facts certainly differs.

The wider spread of Christianity in East Anglia began after Sigibert became king. He had lived for a time as an exile in Gaul and had been converted during his time there. On his accession to the throne, he asked Honorius of Canterbury for help. Honorius sent Felix, a Burgandian missionary who became Bishop of Dunwich. In addition to this help, an Irish monk named Fursa was also welcomed by the king. Fursa established a monastery which had an influence well beyond the borders of East Anglia itself.

Mercia, Middle Anglia and Lindsey became the object of a significant missionary enterprise when, in 653, the son of Penda, a prince named Peada, who was not to become king until the following year, invited four missionaries to come and work in these areas. This development followed the baptism of Peada by Aidan prior to his marriage to Alhflaed, the daughter of Oswiu, then King of Northumbria. Lindsey had benefited from an earlier initiative by Paulinus. While still working in Northumbria, he had conducted missions in Lindsey, the chief town being Lincoln. Paulinus had actually consecrated Honorius as Archbishop of Canterbury in the church in Lincoln as early as 627. Nothing is known of the work of Paulinus in Lindsey after he moved back to Canterbury and we can only assume that the work that remained was consolidated under the later Celtic mission made possible by the invitation of Peada.

The work in Wessex was pioneered by Bishop Birinus who had been consecrated by the Archbishop of Milan. Possibly a German, Birinus baptised the King of Wessex, Cynegils, in 635. Some writers suggest that, because of the origins of Birinus and also because his mission was conducted on the advice of Honorius, the church he established was very much on the Roman model. But even here the position is complex. The work of Birinus was followed by that of Agilbert who was a Frank by birth, but who had studied in Ireland. Though Agilbert accepted the Roman method for dating Easter, so had the Irish monks in the part of Ireland in which he had studied. It is entirely possible that Celtic influences were also present through his work. We can certainly say that large numbers of Irish monks were present in Wessex because of the work of Maildubh who established a notable monastery in Malmesbury.

Even amongst the East Saxons the work of the Celts was evident. Shortly after the middle of the century, Sigibert, King of the East Saxons, was persuaded by Oswiu of Northumbria, the brother of and successor to Oswald, to become a Christian. Oswiu asked the Celtic missionary Cedd, who had earlier been part of the mission to the Middle Angles, to work amongst the East Saxons.

Even amongst the South Saxons, where the Anglo-Saxon Wilfred, tireless opponent of the Celtic church, is honoured as the local apostle of Sussex, Celtic influence is evident. The conversion of the South Saxons was greatly influenced by Diciul, one of Fursa's band of followers. Diciul travelled to Sussex around the year 645 and in time converted the king. He was followed in his work by Wilfred.

Clearly there had been a shift in influence during this first half of the seventh century. At the beginning of the century, the Celts from Iona were not even present in England, while the mission at Canterbury was finding favour in many places throughout England. By the time of the death of Honorius, the last of Augustine's companions, in 652, the archbishopric in Canterbury had no direct influence beyond the boundaries of Kent itself.

But this reversal of fortunes was not to last for long. The Synod of Whitby in 664, at which the differences between the Celtic and Roman missions were debated, marked a dramatic shift in the influence of Canterbury as compared with that of the very active Celts. It is not that Celtic missions ceased at that point, although a number of monks associated with Lindisfarne did return to Iona and Ireland following their defeat at Whitby. Irish monks continued to work widely in England until they were specifically excluded by the Council of Celchyth (Chelsea) in 816. Whitby should be thought of as a political victory for Canterbury which had a long-term significance, rather than acting as an indication of the impact of the respective missions.

Until recently, the dominant view of historians seemed to be that the influence of the Celts was temporary and short-lived. In such a view the victory of the Romans at Whitby was inevitable, representing a gradual and necessary consolidation of the rather haphazard approach of the wandering Celts. Within this broader tradition some have maintained that it is simply impossible to untangle the two influences, that the practical evidence seemed to suggest both Celts and Romans worked well together and that in any case it doesn't really matter who was working where. More recent opinion goes so far as to claim that the Celts were the main evangelists of England with the Romans making a minor, or at least junior, partner contribution. The more recent view, that the Celts were far more important in the conversion of England than previously understood, suggests that earlier views are simply the story told from the perspective of the victor. Viewed from this perspective, even the Saxon Bede, who was sympathetic to the Roman view, had to acknowledge the importance of the Celts.

What can we make of such diverse views? There is little doubt that the evidence is confusing. Certainly at times the two traditions did seem to work together in the same geographic area. But it is also true that the differences in practice seemed to matter to a degree that makes a broader co-operative pattern a puzzle. Perhaps the real truth is that the Roman and Celtic missions were pursuing parallel agendas. These were not mutually exclusive but they were certainly different. In very simple terms we can say that the Celtic missionaries were abbots, while the Roman missionaries were bishops. This single difference points to some very different understandings of the church and the nature of the missionary task.

Of course, we can find Romans who were abbots and Celts who became bishops, but in general terms the Roman missionaries did seem to be more concerned with the ecclesial authority that stemmed from the establishment of a bishopric, even when a monastery was attached, whereas the Celts seemed more concerned to establish monasteries even when a bishop was attached to the monastery. As noted earlier, Columba was never a bishop and yet was clearly the dominant figure in Scotland. Celtic heroes in England, such as Cuthbert, became bishops, but were anxious to be ascetics, even hermits, rather than to exercise diocesan authority. It is some of these differences that later chapters will document in more detail.

CELTS ON THE CONTINENT

Following the collapse of the Roman Empire, particularly because of the arrival of a whole range of broadly Germanic peoples primarily in central and western Europe, but extending as far south as parts of Italy, the situation for the Christian community was rather complicated. In general terms, Christian communities continued to survive in the towns bounded by the former Roman Empire. Some of these communities were known for their learning and holiness. In particular, centres such as Poitiers and Tours produced notable Christian scholars and leaders.

There were some signs of hope for the church. Clovis, one of the foremost Frankish kings, was baptised and so to some degree the Catholic church was able to extend its influence in the territories ruled by him and his successors. But the spiritual life of the church was often weak and its leaders corrupt. Moreover, even when the newcomers adopted the faith it was not always the Catholic version. A good number of the tribes in central and eastern Europe had adopted the Arian heresy.[8] To make matters worse, Christianity was usually confined to

---

[8] See Rowan Williams, *Arius* (DLT, 1987).

the towns. Indeed, the very word 'pagan' originally meant 'country dweller'. Christianity was either weak or non-existent in rural areas and, in the new order, many began to leave the decaying towns for the pagan countryside. The Celts were to become a potent missionary force in the process of converting the new Europeans to Christianity.

Before Aidan arrived in Northumbria, Celtic missionaries were journeying to various parts of the mainland of Europe. Many of these early journeys were centred on the frequent travels of missionaries from Wales, Cornwall and Ireland to Brittany. These natural contacts with other Celtic communities were soon expanded by the travels of many others, mostly Irish monks to parts of western, southern, central and eastern Europe. For at least five hundred years a tide of missionaries established monasteries in France, Germany, Switzerland, Austria, Italy and as far east as the Ukraine.

By far the most notable of these missionaries was the monk Columbanus. He was born in Ireland around 543 and trained first at a monastery near Lough Erne in Sligo under Sinell. From there he received further training at Bangor and eventually left Ireland in 591 travelling with twelve companions to France. Eventually he established a notable monastery at Luxeuil in eastern France where a community of at least six hundred monks lived and worked. From here his reputation spread far and wide. Columbanus encouraged his monks to establish other monasteries following the same very strict rule that he established at Luxeuil. By the end of the seventh century at least ninety-four monasteries had been established which owed their origin either directly or indirectly to his work.

The rather forthright manner of Columbanus in taking the royal family to task over their morals eventually led to his expulsion from that part of France, and he began a journey which took him first to Switzerland where he established a monastery in the town and canton of St Gall. Opposition from the same royal family which had expelled him from France caused him to move once more. His renewed travels led eventually to Bobbio in northern Italy where he founded a third monastery.

The influence of Columbanus on the emerging Christian life of Europe was sufficiently great that some modern Europeans regard him as the patron saint of Europe. This impact was felt in terms of the preaching of the gospel, the flowering of scholarship, the training of thousands of monks and a profound influencing of many in royal households. A good number of those who eventually found themselves working in England had in fact been trained in one or other of the monasteries founded by Columbanus. Thus, in a rather indirect manner, the Celtic influence of religious life on England as well as many continental lands was greater than is at first realised.

Although the work of Columbanus and other Celts was often reinforced by Saxon missionaries such as Boniface, who was rather opposed to the work of Columbanus, the overall impact of the Irish missions was to move the impact of the gospel into the areas of pagan influence in the countryside, which an older urban-based Christianity had failed to accomplish. Most of the Irish foundations eventually went over to the Benedictine rule after a period of one or two hundred years. A small number, such as the one at Peronne, remained entirely Irish for many hundreds of years. But even as the majority took on a Benedictine rule, the flavour of monastic life in Europe had been profoundly influenced. The laxity and even immorality which had been far too prevalent prior to the arrival of the Irish was decisively reformed. The pagan invaders of Europe had met with a force of Christian missionaries whose zeal and devotion represented a spiritual power to be reckoned with.

4

THE MONASTERY IN MISSION

At first sight it might seem curious that an institution which is never mentioned in the Bible and in fact had no place in the life of the early church, should come to exercise such a key role in the evangelisation of Europe. For the Western world, mission was monasticism and monasticism was mission. The monastery was the centre of culture, civilisation and mission.[1] The Western world had two primary forms of monastic life through the period that we call the Dark Ages. The Celtic and Benedictine forms emerged and existed side by side throughout much of western Europe during this period. In order to understand how this situation arose it is vital to have in mind a brief overview of the origins and development of the monastic movement.

---

[1] See David Bosch, *Transforming Mission: Paradigm Shifts in Theology of Mission* (Orbis Books, 1992), p. 230.

THE ORIGINS OF MONASTICISM[2]

The origins of monasticism contain a number of paradoxes. We associate monasticism with community life and yet it did not begin with community. Monasticism became the centre of mission in the West and yet it did not begin with a concern for mission in any accepted sense of the word. Monasticism became a key civilising centre for the whole of western society and yet it did not begin in the west but in the east.

Where and why did the monastic tradition begin? It is no coincidence that monks first emerged in the very parts of the world where Christianity was widely embraced by society. Following the official warmth of the Roman Empire towards Christianity after the Edict of Milan in 313, large numbers of people joined the church.[3] While no doubt some of these were devout converts who heard the word more easily in an atmosphere of open tolerance, there were clearly many who saw it as serving their personal interests to join the church. One contemporary observer lamented:

The doctrines of the Fathers are despised, the speculation of innovators hold sway in the Church ... the

---

[2] See Bernard McGinn and John Meyendorff (eds.), *Christian Spirituality: Origins to the Twelfth Century* (Routledge & Kegan Paul, 1986), ch. 5, and Jordan Aumann, *Christian Spirituality in the Catholic Tradition* (Ignatius Press, 1985), for clear and concise readings on the origins of monasticism.

[3] The Edict of Milan was a proclamation by Constantine and his then ally Licinius to tolerate both Christian and pagan worship as equal. Constantine went on to split with Licinius and favour the Christians, winning battles in the name of the Lord. See Diarmaid MacCulloch, *Groundwork of Christian History* (Epworth Press, 1987), pp. 87–8.

wisdom of this world has the place of honour having dispossessed the boasting of the Cross. The shepherds are driven out; in their place grievous wolves are brought in which harry the flock. Houses of prayer have none to assemble in them; the deserts are full of mourners.[4]

One reaction to the partial introduction of a new worldliness to the community of the church was for some to move to the deserts of Syria and Egypt; there to seek a spiritual life unsullied by the compromises of what some saw as an increasingly degenerate church. This process began in the second half of the fourth century – within a single generation of Constantine's new policy of toleration. In truth it built on some older traditions within the church.

From very early times the church had encouraged those who were single women, either because they had never married or because their husbands had died or divorced them, to work in the service of the church. Such service meant that often the church supported these women. Some were encouraged to offer practical service to the congregation and some to devote themselves to prayer. As time went by, this separated life of devotion sometimes took on an ascetic ingredient. Men as well as women aspired to a life of prayer and asceticism and the numbers of these grew within many congregations.

Moreover, times of persecution meant that some became martyrs. We cannot be certain, but there is a strong possibility that the tradition of asceticism and prayer produced the

---

[4] Oliver Davies and Fiona Bowie, *Celtic Christian Spirituality* (SPCK, 1995), p. 134.

training ground for those who were willing to stand as martyrs. The coming of official tolerance meant an end to the possibility of martyrdom and threatened to a degree the respect the congregation accorded prayer and asceticism. These could easily be looked on as the attributes of fanatics who were the necessary lifeblood of the church in difficult times, but looked curiously out of place in the new situation. It doesn't take much imagination to see how men and women such as these would move from the congregation to the desert partly as protest at the new worldliness and partly to be faithful to their own sense of spiritual devotion. The new monks represented both consciously and unconsciously an older tradition of martyrdom. At first, some of the bishops actively persecuted this new movement, seeing it as operating outside the authority of the church. How ironic that the first monks had to escape the church as much as the world!

The first monks were hermits and so the movement was essentially individualistic. Their inspiration is usually thought to be Anthony of Egypt who was born into a Christian family about 251.[5] When only eighteen he gave up all that he had in order to live a life of prayer and asceticism. Gradually his fame spread, so that eventually great crowds flocked to be with him in his isolation! The result of this tension was that he fled further and further into the desert in order to find solitude. But people still sought him out. In time he accepted an organisational solution which allowed other monks to build cells near his, thus creating a kind of community of hermits. The monks congregated together for worship and celebration of the

---

[5] See James Wellard, *Desert Pilgrimage: A Journey into Christian Egypt* (Hutchinson, 1970), for a good account of the life of St Anthony of Egypt and desert monasticism.

Eucharist on Saturdays and Sundays while living separately on the remaining days.

A more consciously communitarian form of monasticism also developed in Egypt. Its pioneer was Pachomius who was born of pagan parents in Egypt around the year 292. Following his conversion, he went to live with a hermit for seven years, after which, in 323, he gathered a group of around a hundred followers and established a community of monks with a conscious rule of life. Pachomius died in 346 by which time he had established eleven monasteries (nine for men and two for women). As many as seven thousand people lived in these centres.

The vigour of this new monastic tradition began to spread throughout the East, into Mesopotamia, Syria, Cappadocia and into North Africa. This spread coincided with the arrival of another new tradition, that of pilgrimage to the Holy Land[6]. Although there had always been a few pilgrims, as far back as Mellito of Sardis, who visited the Holy Land in the year 170, the flood of pilgrims did not really begin until after the restoration of the holy sites by Constantine, inspired as he was by the visit of his mother to Palestine. Pilgrims to the Holy Land often received hospitality from the various monastic communities. Moreover, some went to the Holy Land by way of Egypt and Gaza and took time to visit monasteries as they went. Although the monastic ideal was beginning to spread to the West, especially because bishops in the West were beginning

---

[6] See Martin Robinson, *Sacred Places, Pilgrimage Paths: An Anthology of Pilgrimage* (HarperCollins, 1997), for a good overview of pilgrimage narratives including the Holy Land and for an extensive bibliography of Holy Land pilgrimage sources.

to recognise monasticism's value, the flow of pilgrims certainly assisted its transfer westwards.

Without question, the first monastic centre in the West was that established by Martin of Tours.[7] His first centre was established around 360 in Poitiers and after his accession to the bishopric of Tours in 372 he founded a second monastery close to the city of Tours at Marmoutiers. But the transition of monasticism to the West brought some subtle changes. In some respects the tradition begun by St Martin was rather like the example of St Anthony in Egypt in that a number of monks lived in separate cells coming together only to worship and eat. Their strict fasting and copying of manuscripts also echoed Anthony's earlier example.

But there were at least two key differences between Martin and Anthony. First, Martin was a scholar and he used the monastic communities that he founded to develop the discipline of learning. In a world which was just beginning to lose contact with the ancient inheritance of Greece and Rome, Martin was able to preserve some connection with an ancient tradition of scholarship. Second, Martin was concerned to link the monastic life with mission. In one sense, even the tradition of Anthony was concerned for mission through his emphasis on prayer for purity. But the context was rather different. Anthony lived in a world where the majority were at least nominally Christian and needed to be encouraged to take their spiritual life more seriously. Martin lived in a world where the majority had never been Christians. The Christian community lived in an urban context and the countryside was still almost

<hr>

[7] See Christopher Donaldson, *Martin of Tours: The Shaping of Celtic Spirituality* (Routledge, 1980).

entirely pagan. Preaching missions to the country areas formed an important part of Martin's agenda.

It was the model of Martin of Tours that was transmitted to the Celtic lands of Britain and Ireland. This is clearly the case with the Candida Casa of Ninian (360–432), which was explicitly modelled on the work of Martin. Ninian is said by many scholars to have visited Martin of Tours on returning from his studies in Rome.[8] Ninian's monastic settlement was dedicated to Martin of Tours who died in 397 at the time when Candida Casa was being constructed. There is no direct evidence that the Welsh foundations of Cadoc and Illtud were modelled after Martin of Tours, but that seems the most likely given both the fame of St Martin and the absence of other available models.

Two stark developments may have combined to assist such a process. First, the Romano-Celtic world of the middle to late fourth century were marked by a sense of crisis. The gradual withdrawal of the protection of the empire produced a feeling that the past was under threat. The gathering together of like-minded Christians in a loose monastic structure offered a link with the past. The learning of Martin of Tours offered a model by which a fading civilisation might be preserved at least in microcosm. Some writers suggest that the first forms of monastery in Wales may have been based around existing Roman villas. A local wealthy family may have felt strengthened at a time of crisis by the presence of such a community.[9]

Second, the dimension of mission found in Martin's model may also have seemed highly appropriate for those who were

---

[8] For example, see J. Hanna, *The History of the Celtic Church* (Edward Brothers, 1962), p. 18.

[9] See Philip Sheldrake, *Living Between Worlds* (DLT, 1995), pp. 13–15.

aware that the Christian faith needed to be taken to those surrounding areas of the countryside which had never become Christian. Martin had become known as one who fearlessly tore down pagan temples and symbols of worship. The minority of Christians in the British Isles may well have wished to emulate his example. A community of devout believers, consecrating themselves in a life of prayer would have seemed far more able to conduct mission in troubled times.

It was these early attempts at formulating a Celtic equivalent to the continental monastic model that took root in Ireland.[10] The theme of preserving a link with a past that had been well formulated was not relevant in an Ireland where Christianity was a relative newcomer. But nonetheless, the perceived strength of Christianity in offering a connection with an older and more developed civilisation could be modelled in a monastic community in a way that a diocesan structure could never manage. This was all the more true in an Ireland which simply did not have the urban context which had fostered diocesan life in other parts of Europe. The urban diocesan structure of the Mediterranean, a bishop for every sizeable town, was hardly appropriate for ministry to a rural, tribal people.[11]

The theme of mission became all-consuming. It was also true that the monastery was much more able than a diocesan structure to train the missionaries who were needed to carry the faith to the tribal structures of Ireland. The monastery therefore took on the task of challenging and reshaping the society to which the mission of the church was directed.

---

[10] See L. Bitel, *Isle of the Saints* (Cornell University Press, 1990), for a wonderful account of the monastic community in Ireland.

[11] See W.H.C. Frend, *The Early Church* (SCM Press, 1965), p. 111.

The emerging monasteries of Ireland were often composed of large numbers of people. Not only were there significant numbers of monks in each monastery, but the support structures necessary to allow such numbers of people to live and work together meant that the monasteries were often the closest structure that Irish society had to a town or city. Many of the larger communities were actually known as cities, for example the 'city of Brigid' for Kildare. The size and role of these communities meant that their relationship with the surrounding social and political structures in society was of great importance.

TRANSFORMING SOCIETY

The Celtic industry of recent years tends to convey a rather romantic view of ancient Celtic society. The truth was that existence on the western shores of Europe was rather precarious and certainly primitive in many respects. Deriving a living from the land was hard indeed. The missionary task demanded tough individuals who could survive in unfavourable physical circumstances. The monastic life fostered such missionaries. But how did they tackle their missionary task?

In the Ireland of St Patrick's day, the basis of society was the extended family which acted as a tribal unit known as the *tuath*, which consisted of the various units of an extended family together with other workers, and sometimes slaves. There were no towns as such. Rather, this was a rural pattern of isolated farmsteads defended by a bank system encircling the houses. We might describe such a settlement as a simple ring fort or *rath*.

The houses were simple in structure using basic local materials. The king or chief might live in a settlement that was larger than those of the other farmsteads in his *tuath*. This would show some signs of greater wealth since the warriors needed to be supported and the king was able to demand the payment of some tributes from the various units within the tribe or clan who owed allegiance to him. There might also be a larger hall used for banqueting and special feasts, but even the king's settlement never approached the status of a town.

Irish society had a number of strata below the king. First were the noblemen who largely represented the warrior class. Second were the literati (brehons [lawyers], druids and bards) and the craftsmen (*aes dana* or 'gifted people'). This group, while valued for the contribution, were nevertheless dependent on the noblemen for patronage. Next came the landowning commoners and, finally, those who provided work for the landowners: labourers, serfs and slaves.

As with many tribal societies, wealth was measured in terms of cattle. (A female slave was considered to be worth three heifers.[12]) In the absence of coinage, trading and other transactions were conducted by barter. The fortunes of the various small kingdoms depended heavily on a combination of the wisdom of their chief, their ability to defend themselves in times of conflict and the dynastic marriages and alliances that were formed. Although in theory all the kings owed allegiance to the High King of Ireland, this did not apply to every kingdom in Ireland and it is questionable as to how much power the high king actually held.

The degree of stability in Irish society might at first sight seem surprising given the absence of a central political organisation. However, stability seems to have come largely from

---

[12] Alannah Hopkin, *The Living Legend of St Patrick* (Grafton Books, 1989), p. 20.

cultural and religious sources. Respect for, and perhaps occasionally fear of, law, the wisdom of the druids and the traditions contained in the songs and poetry of the bards, brought a strong degree of cultural cohesion. If it is true that pagan Ireland was dominated by belief in omens and soothsaying and in the power of curses, magic formulae and sacred places, then it is easy to see how the brehons, druids and bards exercised an influence that few men, kings or not, might like to question. In such a situation, to break law or tradition might be to incur bad luck and in the sometimes tenuous situation of most rural communities, bad luck exhibited in disease amongst people or cattle, might mean disaster.

How then did the new monastic communities relate to an existing tribal and pagan society? Clearly, the monasteries represented both a threat and a potential resource for existing kings. In the early period, the monks were dependent on royal patronage for land and to some degree for protection. In this regard it was helpful that so many of the early saints were themselves the sons of kings, in some cases from Wales. Their social standing, quite apart from any religious status, meant that they needed to be dealt with courteously. The sons of kings knew how to behave in the company of another royal family. They were at ease. Moreover, they had something to offer. They brought news of a world beyond that of Ireland, connections with the wider Celtic diaspora as well as with the ancient civilisations of Greece and Rome. The wanderings of many monks meant that not a few could tell moving tales of life in Egypt, the Holy Land and Galatia in Asia Minor. In time they brought libraries and learning and all this in a cultural framework that was very close to the culture of Celtic Ireland. These were men and women to be taken seriously.

The kings of Ireland were very ready to use this resource in
the education of their own children. It is no accident that, as
Patrick tells us, 'the sons and daughters of the kings of the Irish
are seen to be monks and virgins of Christ'. The influence
and inspiration that flowed from monastic life brought many
recruits from the ranks of royals to be adventurers for Christ.
All that the offspring of the kings needed could be found within the walls of the monastic community. One eleventh-century
poem gives a flavour of the range of positions present within
monastic life, presenting a picture of a highly complex society:

> Psalm-singer, beginning student, historian who is not
>   insignificant,
> instructor, teacher of ecclesiastical law, head teacher
>   with great knowledge.
> Bishop, priest and deacon, subdeacon, a noble course,
>   lector, porter, swift exorcist,
> the holy man is renowned.
> Erenagh, his assistant, vice-abbot, cook, proper and
>   right, counsellor, steward, alternate vice-abbot ...[13]

From the perspective of the kings, the role of the monks was
seen as being closer to that of the literati than to any other
grouping with society. In a sense, the monks fulfilled the role
of brehon, druid and bard. The most obvious group to fear the
coming of Christianity were the druids. Their position had
been strongly reinforced in Irish society by the prescription

---

[13] From Kuno Meyer, *Mitteilungen aus irischen Handschriften* (ZCP 5, 1905),
pp. 498–9; also cited in L. Bitel, *Isle of the Saints* (Cornell University Press,
1990), p. 138.

against the writing down of tradition. The religious traditions of the druids had to be committed to memory and faithfully transmitted to future generations.

Clearly, this was a highly complex task that required a great deal of training and was not undertaken lightly. This specialist skill was highly regarded. The coming of the monks with their challenge to the prohibition of writing down that which was sacred was as critical as the clash of religious ideas themselves. The people of the book represented a profound threat to those whose stock in trade lay in a world of hidden knowledge. The power of the guild was broken once any tradition was written down in a way that could then be referred to by those who had not undergone the same training. Once religious ideas were written down, power resided in the strength of the religious ideas themselves rather than in the power represented by introduction to the world of secrets remembered.

The evidence from Ireland is that there was not a great deal of hostility and certainly no record of a violent encounter between Christianity and pagan religion. Indeed, scholars have made the point that many pagan traditions were easily incorporated into the new Christian tradition. Sacred places and pagan festivals were easily given Christian characteristics. We cannot know how many druids became monks but it would be surprising if some did not. Certainly, we know that Columba had been a druid at one time.

The position of the brehons is also unclear. It seems that they gradually slipped from sight, with well-known abbots effectively fulfilling their role especially in the settling of disputes both military, social and political. Once again, it is possible that a good number of the brehons joined the monasteries but little direct evidence is available. However, we do have good evidence for the role of Columba in settling a key dispute, this time in relation to the position of the bards.

When Columba left Ireland for his mission to Scotland, the circumstances of his departure were such that he had vowed never to set foot on Irish soil again. Towards the end of his life, a series of disputes arose in Ulster and Columba was invited to take part in settling them. Tradition tells us that he wore turfs of Scottish soil on his feet to avoid his feet touching Irish soil. Whether or not this is true, it is certainly the case that he returned to Ireland. We have already mentioned the issue of the tribute paid by the Scots to the Irish. Two other questions were also on the agenda. One issue concerned the position of a particular hostage and does not concern us here.

The last and most difficult question surrounded the position of the bards.[14] Their number had increased and many still held to their pagan traditions at a time when most of the kings and many of the people had become Christians. Their numbers and their behaviour was such that the high king wished to have them banished. Perhaps surprisingly, Columba took the side of the bards. His suggestion was that where they were willing, they should either be given land on which to settle or be allowed to enter the monasteries. The high king agreed to Columba's suggestions and those who went into the monasteries were helped by the monks to write down their songs and poetry. Their gifts and traditions were used in the service of the gospel. It is likely that some became monks. The incorporation of the bards marked the final replacement of the brehons, druids and the bardic class by the monasteries. The potential conflict was resolved.

[14] For more on bards see Ian Finlay, *Columba* (Chambers, 1979), pp. 155–8.

The model of the Irish church which had adapted itself so well to the tribal pattern of Irish society was to prove highly effective in communicating with Anglo-Saxon society. Although Celtic and Saxon culture differed in many respects, it was similar in its tribal structure. Saxon kings in England may well have been more politically and militarily powerful than the high kings of Ireland, but the basic structure of Celtic and Saxon societies were more akin to one another than either was to the urban structures of the earlier Romano-British culture. The class of brehon, druid and bard was not nearly as well-defined or powerful in Saxon culture, which was probably fortunate for the new Christian missions. The power of the Saxon kings was such that they could not be overawed by the early presence of monastic settlements. For this reason, nearly all of the early Celtic missions were highly dependent for their early establishment on the patronage of the king. We have already noted the critical role of the Christian kings of Northumbria in inviting Celtic mission and their role in the establishment of monastic communities, as Bede's *History* reminds us:

> Churches were built in several places, and the people flocked gladly to hear the word of God, while the king of his bounty gave lands and endowments to establish monasteries, and the English, both noble and simple, were instructed by their Scots teachers to observe a monastic life.[15]

Once they were established, the monasteries exercised the same kind of attraction for Saxon nobility as they had in

---

[15] Bede, *A History of the English Church and People* (Penguin, 1988), III, 3.

Ireland. (Although there were more monasteries than convents at this time, the term monastery should be taken to
include convents where they existed, either as separate houses
or as double houses alongside monasteries.) These were centres
of learning at a time when education was a remote possibility
for most of Saxon society. Those who lived within them had a
reputation for holiness, asceticism and the life of prayer, which
brought its own appeal. Moreover, their ability through hard
work, discipline and skill to bring back into productive use a
landscape which had been devastated by invasion won the
respect of nobles and peasants alike.[16] Their commitment to
poverty and charity won the hearts of the poor as much as it
excited the devotion of royals. Their mission was not just to
win individuals to the Christian message but by modelling a
new set of moral and social values to reshape the whole of society in a Christian image. Their purpose was both to cast a
vision which would capture the imagination of a whole society,
and to live out that vision in practical demonstration.

The monasteries produced a wide range of strengths in
terms of their interaction with society. They attracted large
numbers of monks. The inheritance of their tradition meant
that they enjoyed a wealth of wisdom. They became sufficiently well regarded by society as a whole that they could attract to
their number many from noble birth.

THE LIFE OF THE COMMUNITY

The early monasteries in Egypt and during the time of Martin
of Tours were rather informal in the sense that the main reason

---

[16] See David Bosch, *Transforming Mission* (Orbis Books, 1990), p. 232.

for their existence lay in the simple desire of those who lived as monks to be near the spiritual teacher that they had sought out. Athanasius describes his experiences:

> For we know bishops that drink no wine and monks that do ... Many bishops are not married; and on the other hand many monks are fathers of children, and monks that are not so; clergy that eat and drink and monks that fast. For these things are at liberty, and no prohibition laid upon them. Every one exercises himself as he pleases, for it is not men's stations, but their actions, for which they shall be crowned.[17]

The Celtic monasteries of Ireland began to evolve much stricter rules that monks and nuns were expected to keep. There was not a single rule; rather, each community evolved its own rules even if various communities influenced one another. A person entering a monastery or convent was meant to leave family behind and view the community as their new family. Traditional cultural ties of kinship, obligation and even of inheritance were transferred to the new family. The novice was expected to choose a 'soul friend', the *anamchara* in Ireland and the *periglour* in Wales.[18] The soul friend was tutor, mentor and confessor. The relationship involved a high degree

---

[17] From a letter to the monk Draconitius, cited in Leslie Hardinge, *The Celtic Church in Britain* (SPCK, 1972), p. 155.

[18] According to both the rules of St Carthage and St Columba, the hierarchical relationship between junior monks and their senior mentor or soul friends was most important. Indeed, Columba's rule indicates that the junior monk should confess daily to his soul friend.

of affection and closeness. The role of the abbot was rather more distant and paternal.

Celibacy was regarded as the ideal but was not compulsory. Some within the monastery had families which they continued to support. It was not impossible for monks or nuns to return to be with their families from time to time. On occasion the son or nephew of an abbot might be looked to as the natural successor to the abbot's position.

The relationship of the community to the land was just as important as it was for the rural society which characterised the society of the day. In the early development of the monasteries, the community would generally expect to support itself entirely by the produce which it grew rather than by receiving any form of tithe or tribute. Indeed, the skill, patient determination and disciplined hard work which characterised the agricultural approach of many monasteries was one element in the respect which the monks eventually earned both in Celtic and Saxon society.

The very first monastic communities had to work land that had not been used before. As the usefulness of the monasteries began to be appreciated by society more widely, gifts of land became more common. Sometimes these gifts were given as part of the entry to the monastery of some from noble families. On other occasions they were simply the generous gifts of members of the royal family or from other nobles. The growing size of some communities, together with the need for larger areas of land to support them, brought into being a wider community who were not monks or nuns but had a close relationship to the monastery or convent. Some of these were farmers who were tenants of monastery lands, others were freemen who were related to the community but who owned their own lands, while the community also included some who were not freemen and who provided valuable labour. While it may seem strange for a religious community to have slaves as part of their monastic life, the harshness of the times was such that it may well have been a welcome change for those whose life might otherwise have been much worse. It must not be forgotten that the division of mental and physical labour was a natural distinction as the rule attributed to St Carthach (d. 637) indicates:

> We watch, we read, we pray,
> Each according to his strength ...
> Labour for the illiterate,
> Guided by pious clerics:
> The wise man's work is in his mouth,
> The unlearned work with their hands.[19]

This stanza reminds us that life in a Celtic community was, for many, not quite as rosy as one would tend to imagine! But despite this division of labour and the use of the hands of the 'illiterate' we must not imagine that the manual work performed for the monastic community was undertaken with bitterness. As Adamnan reminds us in the opening chapter of his *Life of Saint Columba*, it was possible to work for the monastery with joy:

> '... and though the load I carry on my back is heavy,
> from here to the monastery it grows light, how I know

---

[19] See Alexander MacEwan, *A History of the Church in Scotland* (Hodder & Stoughton, 1915), I, p. 131; and cited also in John McNeill, *The Celtic Churches: A History AD 200 to 1200* (University of Chicago Press, 1974), p. 81.

not, but I am burdened no longer' ... Baithene replied,
'It is our old master, Columba, mindful of our toil, and
anxious because we are so late home. And, since he
cannot come to meet us in the body, he sends his spirit
to refresh and rejoice us.'[20]

LIVING FOR OTHERS

By its very definition, monastic life represents a call to poverty
and simplicity of lifestyle – the absence of the pursuit of the
material, in order to concentrate better on the spiritual life. It
would be possible for those who have ceased to be concerned
for the material to be blind to the material needs of others. Yet
the Christian practice of spirituality has rarely taken such a
path. Service towards and compassion for the poor, the out-
cast, the suffering and the needy has always been an integral
part of the spiritual life for Christians of all traditions.

In the case of the Celtic saints, their concern for the poor
became a significant feature of their ministry and renown. This
aspect of their life is discussed in more detail in Chapter 9. The
stories of their generosity towards the poor are numerous, characterised by the occasion when the king gave Aidan a fine
horse, for urgent or difficult journeys, only to find that Aidan
gave it to the next poor person whom he met, such was his
compassion for others.

When this action came to the king's ears, he asked the
bishop as they were going to dine: 'My lord bishop,

---

[20] Adamnan, *Life of St Columba*, trans. William Reeves (Llanerch
Enterprises, 1988).

why did you give away the royal horse which was necessary for your own use? Have we not many less valuable horses which would have been good enough for beggars, without giving away a horse that I had specially selected for your personal use?' The bishop at once answered, 'What are you saying, Your Majesty? Is this child of a mare more valuable to you than this child of God?'[21]

The way these stories are told is as important as the content itself. The point of many of these stories is not to highlight the greatness of the saint so much as to explain and illustrate the affection of the poor for these roaming Celtic monks and nuns. Often the most able saints were from wealthy and privileged backgrounds and yet their concern for the poor was sufficiently great to endear the poor to them. The monastic community strove for an ideal in which all were equal, even to the degree that Pope Gregory, in the spirit of Cuthbert's model on Lindisfarne, wrote to Augustine:

You, brother, have been brought up in the monastic rule. Now that the faith has been brought to the English you must not start living apart from your clergy. Introduce that way of life practised by the fathers of the early church, none of whom claimed as his own anything he possessed – for everything was held in common.[22]

---

[21] Bede, *History*, III, 14.

[22] From Bede's *Life of St Cuthbert*, ch. 16, in *The Age of Bede*, trans. J.F. Webb, ed. D.H. Farmer (Penguin, 1965), and also Bede's *History*, I, 27.

An awareness of a special responsibility for others extended also to the sphere of hospitality. The motivation for such concern flowed from their understanding of the spiritual life as illustrated by these lines from the Liber ex Lege Moisi:[23]

> O king of stars!
> Whether my house be dark or bright,
> Never shall it be closed against any one,
> Lest Christ close his house against me.
>
> If there be a guest in your house
> And you conceal aught from him,
> 'Tis not the guest who will be without,
> But Jesus, Mary's Son.[24]

Hospitality in general was seen as an important obligation for a monastic house. The rule of Ailbe suggests that the monastic community should supply 'a clean house for the guests and a big fire, washing and bathing for them, and a couch without sorrow'.[25] To some extent, the hospitality of the Celtic houses was a reflection of the general view of hospitality in Celtic culture. But the motives were rather different. In secular life the claim of hospitality and the care with which it was exercised was a matter of honour in fulfilling duty and to some extent carried an implicit claim about the wealth of the tribe. For the monks the obligation had more to do with the imitation of

---

[23] The Liber ex Lege Moisi is what one might call a Celtic 'book of law'.

[24] Cited in Hardinge, The Celtic Church in Britain, p. 176.

[25] Cited in Kathleen Hughes, The Church in Early Irish Society (Methuen, 1966), p. 148.

Christ. This is reflected in the care that they took not to con-
sume as much food as the laity or to be seen in any way as
a glutton. To imitate Christ is to live for others, it is also to
be acutely aware of the nature of the spiritual battle. Their
constant self-denial was a means of perfecting their spiritual
discipline. Prolonged periods of prayer and self-inflicted physical hardship served the same purpose. Chapter 9 explores this
aspect of their community life in more detail.

The frequent self-denial as well as the tough penances
imposed on monks and nuns might seem unduly harsh to us.
Certainly, much contemporary writing on Celtic spirituality
is strangely quiet on the matter of physical penance and
endurance. Apart from prolonged periods of fasting, silence,
repeated genuflections and reduction of sleep, the discipline
could also include corporal punishment.[26]

But such a life needs to be seen within its context. The
monks and nuns understood themselves to be soldiers of
Christ. Their self-mortification was designed to help them
to withstand the attacks of the evil one which were seen as
potentially much more hazardous than self-denial or even
physical pain. Their role in this kind of spiritual warfare was to
overcome spiritual barriers and so to enable the gospel to be
spread. In this sense they saw themselves as acting to help society at large by defeating evil on these spiritual frontiers.

Moreover, even apart from the issue of spiritual prepared-
ness, life outside the monastery was also harsh. The life of the
community was not to be seen as an escape from the world to a
life of ease but as a preparation for mission. Life generally was

---

[26] James Mackey, *Introduction to Celtic Christianity* (T. & T. Clark, 1993),
p. 107.

tough and those who wanted to engage the respect of those to whom they went needed to demonstrate a flinty resolve. This was not an ancient version of Victorian 'muscular Christianity' so much as a quality of spirit illustrated by an ability to withstand deprivation and hardship. The very same qualities were much prized by those who were warriors in the secular world.

It is difficult to avoid the conclusion that part of the reason for the success of the Celts as missionaries lay in the deep respect with which they were held. Their toughness of resolve and purpose suggested that these were people with a message that needed to be taken seriously. Their physical endurance, empowered by God, outdid the physical prowess of the strongest warriors. These men and women could be admired even if their actions sometimes seemed puzzling. Their lives in community authenticated the message. Their commitment to the poor, the weak and the deprived which flowed from their own strength of purpose seemed to bear witness to the power of the message.

5

SPIRITUALITY AND MISSION

 The notion that the monastery lay at the heart of the mission, that the abbot was in fact the spiritual director of the bishop, suggests not just a difference of ecclesiology but also a different approach to spirituality. The two clearly impact one another and are easily confused. Nowhere is this better illustrated than in the clash between the Roman and Celtic parties at Whitby. The conflict is often seen as representing the triumph of one form of ecclesiology over another. Certainly, it was external forms surrounding acts of worship that were discussed but these were only symbolic of deeper conflict.

The debate between the Celtic and Roman missionaries at the Synod of Whitby highlighted the fact that there were clear differences between the Roman church and the Celtic church in the matter of worship. Although there were other differences also, for example in relation to the matter of the tonsure, dress, episcopal consecration and the issue of bishops without a specific jurisdiction, the matter of worship tended to produce the greatest degree of passion. There were five obvious differences between the two factions.

The first, and most contentious, concerned the dating of Easter. The debate at Whitby focused on the fact that Celtic and Roman practice produced a different system for arriving at the date of the Easter celebration. Differences on this issue had been present for some time and in addition to the Roman and Celtic systems for dating Easter, there was also the Alexandrian and Quartodeciman systems.[1] The question was sufficiently complex that the popes prior to the seventh century had never made any particular ruling as to which system should be used although there was a tendency for the Quartodeciman system to be condemned (following the Council of Nicaea), because of its Jewish connection. Indeed, the lack of strong agreement on this issue for so many centuries makes it all the more surprising that it should suddenly have emerged as an issue at all. Some have speculated that it did so partly because of the coincidence that the two western systems for calculating Easter happened to produce the same dates over a significant period in the early seventh century, given an appearance of uniformity, and that these dates were dramatically different from the date of Easter as celebrated by the Celts. The suspicion that this issue was merely a convenient debating device is reinforced by the fact of Pope Gregory's failure to comment on Columbanus' Celtic practice on this matter.

The notion that this was mostly a debating device is further strengthened by the fact that although the controversy centred on Easter, the Celtic and Roman churches had wide differences in practice in relation to the celebration of a number of festivals. For example, the Celts followed the Eastern practice of celebrating Christmas on Epiphany rather than on 25 December. The Celts usually had three major fast periods:

---

[1] See W.H.C. Frend, *The Early Church* (SCM Press, 1965), p. 76, and Ian Hazlett (ed.), *Early Christianity* (SPCK, 1991), p. 199.

Lent, the forty days prior to Christmas and the forty days immediately after Whitsun as compared with the single Roman fast of Lent. The Celts did not celebrate the various feasts connected with saints' days in the way that the Roman church did. Why then centre on one festival as compared with many others unless those who chose the ground for the debate simply felt that this was a strong debating point?

In this sense the offence of the Celts in the eyes of the Roman party was not a miscalculation concerning dates but the very act of dissension itself. To agree to comply becomes an act of necessary faith as compared with matters of accuracy relating to the issue itself. As Bede reports the spokesman for the Roman position at Whitby: 'But you and your colleagues are most certainly guilty of sin if you reject the decrees of the Apostolic See, indeed of the universal church, which are conformed by Holy Writ.'[2]

What then was it that was confirmed by the sacred scriptures and confirmed by the universal church? Not the date of Easter so much as the claim of Rome to the authority of Peter.

A second difference between the Roman and Celtic position concerned the actual liturgy surrounding the mass. Unlike the Roman church, the Celts had no single liturgy but instead developed a number of local or regional liturgies, none of which was particularly dominant.[3] Within these different liturgies

---

[2] Bede, A *History of the English Church and People* (Penguin, 1988), III, 25.
[3] The most famous of known liturgies from Celtic lands is the Stowe Missal. This Latin text is a prime example of the point in question as there is really little to distinguish it in content from any other Latin missal to be found anywhere on the Continent at the time.

there were a variety of local customs. For example, foot washing seems to have been widely used in a number of Celtic
liturgies.

A third disagreement, although it did not surface in a
contentious way, was that the Roman church had followed
Constantine's edict in adopting Sunday as the primary day of
worship for the church. The Celts, by contrast, more usually
took Saturday as the special day of weekly worship. This
practice simply reflected the earlier widespread custom of
Sabbatarian worship commonly used in the early church. The
lack of obvious tension over this issue stems partly from
the way in which the day was understood. Some Celts began
the Saturday observance on the Friday evening and continued
it until sunrise on the Sunday. This slightly ambiguous way of
viewing the extent of a single day allowed the possibility of
merging these two traditions.

A fourth difference was that baptism in the Celtic tradition also followed the Eastern practice of full immersion, usually of a triune kind. The Roman tendency was to allow the
use of less water with a single pouring. In the early Celtic tradition, baptism was usually of adults with a service of blessing
being used in relation to infants. However, this tradition
reflected the largely missionary context of the Celtic church
and it seems that infant baptism was introduced prior to the
conflict at Whitby. Other minor differences, such as the suggestion that some candidates were also anointed with oil as
part of the baptismal rite, seem to have been part of more local
traditions. One source implies that on occasion baptism was
performed with milk!

A fifth contrast was that communion was administered by
the Celts in both kinds, as compared with the more normal
Roman practice of administering the bread alone. Columbanus

supposedly issues a warning to those who damaged the chalice with their teeth![4]

At one level these differences mattered very little. There was no implicit or even explicit division of doctrine. It would be possible to view these divergent practices as local matters which might be harmonised over time. Even the potentially awkward and embarrassing disagreement concerning the date of Easter raised no issues concerning the essence of the faith. It has often been noted that the Celtic church in some parts of Britain and Ireland adopted Roman customs without harming the essentially Celtic character of their worship. The debate at Whitby makes it clear that the real issue was not one of custom so much as authority. What was at stake was not just the correct date but far more the question of who had the authority to determine such matters. The gradual adoption of Roman practice reflects the growing authority of Rome, rather than a recognition that the intellectual argument concerning Easter, or any other matter, had been won by the Roman party.

SPIRITUALITY AND WORLDVIEW

The reaction of the Celtic church to the outcome of Whitby reveals that there was one more issue which went deeper even than that of authority. Although it is difficult to express, the spirituality of a community also says something about the worldview of those who engage in worship. The Celtic approach to worship and spirituality, much more than the outward forms of that worship, reflects an underlying understanding of the

---

[4] For a more in-depth exploration of such liturgical practices see ch. 4 of Leslie Hardinge, *The Celtic Church in Britain* (SPCK, 1972).

world. That worldview has as much to do with feeling as it does with definition. The rest of this chapter attempts to illustrate that difference of feeling.

The Place of the Sacred

The relationship between the sacred and the profane in a given society tells us a great deal about worldview. Clearly there are many possible ways of understanding these key concepts. In more recent centuries, there has been a tendency for the Western world to separate the secular and the sacred in such a way that the sacred has become marginalised either because it has been seen as unreal or at best as private.[5] In either configuration, the sacred hardly impacts the public sphere of activity. Sociologists have noted a very recent move towards the resacralisation of some areas of secular life. So, for example, the new interest in ecology has led some to see the natural world as containing a sacred dimension.[6] In such a framework

---

[5] The seminal text on this subject that sparked a whole flurry of explorations around the nature of the sacred and its relation to the 'profane' can be found in Rudolph Otto, *The Idea of the Holy* (OUP, 1923); this volume has recently been published again in paperback, which bears witness to its lasting appeal. Another writer, whose many works deal with this area, is the French anthropologist Mircea Eliade; his works have been translated widely.

[6] Much of the work in this area has been inspired by James Lovelock's Gaia hypothesis. While Lovelock's work is a purely scientific exploration, it has fuelled the imagination of many theologians, especially those already working within the field of theology and gender studies. Some of the most significant texts within this area are as follows: M. Mies and V. Shiva, *Ecofeminism* (Zed Books, 1993); Janet Plant, *Healing the Wounds: The Promise of Ecofeminism* (Green Print, 1989); Anne Primavesi, *From Apocalypse to Genesis: Ecology, Feminism and Christianity* (Burns & Oates, 1991); Rosemary Reuther, *Gaia and God: An Ecofeminist Theology of Earth Healing* (SCM Press, 1993).

the living world is important, not just because it contains important resources for human life, but because it is valuable in its own right.

Some older civilisations chose to separate the sacred and the secular in such a way that they almost occupied parallel universes. In such a system the goal was either to escape or reject the material in order to grasp the spiritual or to find ways of appeasing the potential threat of the spiritual in the material realm. The world of the Old and New Testaments suggests a much more integrated understanding of the material and the spiritual. In this framework the natural world is sacralised by the intent, will and action of the Creator God. The world is sacred because it is God's handiwork. It is this Judaeo-Christian understanding that infuses the world of Celtic Christianity.

Christians generally agree that in principle the world is good because it has been created by a good God. The problem for the Christian in making such a claim is that there are all too many instances where the world seems to be anything but good. Evil has found a place in God's good world. Not only does this seem to be so, but clearly Christians also wish to claim that the created and seen world does not constitute the whole of reality. There is another world towards which we make pilgrimage. Spiritual powers, both malign and good, seek to make their impact on the world of the seen and known. Celtic Christian spirituality had its own response to make to the world of the 'other'.

Sacred Places, Sacred Spaces

There is an inevitable paradox contained within the claim that God is everywhere and yet that some places are special. As one writer has noted, 'it is paradoxical that we should claim that God is everywhere and yet seek him in special places, yet it is a paradox which we, having created, need to accept'.[7] For most Christians sacred places become sacred because of their association with particular people or particular events. Celtic Christians were no different in this respect. Sites associated with saints or with miraculous healings were held to be sacred. But Celtic Christians did not stop with these associations.

Some sacred places represented a continuation of an older pre-Christian tradition. It is not clear whether this was merely a matter of replacing a pagan shrine with a Christian shrine as a matter of convenience or whether there was a deeper significance attached to the places where pagan shrines already existed. In other words, it is possible that certain sites were recognised as containing an intrinsic power that needed to be appropriated for a Christian purpose.

Certain places were seen as important because of their association with a particular natural feature. Some streams or wells were seen as containing healing power even in pre-Christian times. Other sites too, especially related to sacred trees, such as the oak, were seen as significant. There seems also to have been an attachment to high places, hilltops or mountain-tops. But the characteristically different attachment of Celtic Christians as compared with their pagan forerunners, belongs to their interest in secluded or isolated sites, in particular, remote islands.

Some years ago, I visited a cave, said to have been the home of one of the saints who worked in Wales. The inaccessibility of the place struck me. Even in the twentieth century, with a road to take one part of the way, finding the cave was

[7] Shirley Du Boulay, *The Road to Canterbury* (HarperCollins, 1994), pp. 6–7.

extraordinarily difficult. Part of the problem sprang from the fact that it was near the top of a substantial hill. (Someone brought up in Scotland is reluctant to call it a mountain.) The guidebook in the local church dedicated to the saint in question suggested that this Irish ascetic chose his cave because it was possible to look across to Ireland. I have to say that I saw no sign of Ireland on the day I climbed the hill but in any case I wondered whether that was the real reason for his choice.

It also occurred to me that this was a strange missionary strategy – to go as far away from the centres of population as possible and to trust that those who needed to hear the gospel would seek you out in this remote wilderness. There would be few from the Church Growth school of thought who would recommend such an approach!

Admittedly, it is true that many who sought to be ascetics, men such as Cuthbert, were renowned not only for the times they spent in remote isolation but also for their missionary travels. Therefore, one could argue that it was not the case that they only waited in the wilderness for others to find them. It is also true that many did seek out such saints. Their reputation for holiness, wisdom, prayer and the miraculous acted as a spiritual magnet to the point where visitors sometimes became something of a problem.

What was it that created this missionary paradigm? There is an obvious relationship between the wilderness of the Celt and the desert of the Egyptian monastics that had inspired the Celtic church. One writer has noted that 'in the Celtic lands quite a number of traditional Christian sites are commemorated in modern place names by the various local words for "desert".'[8]

---

[8] Philip Sheldrake, *Living Between Worlds* (DLT, 1995), p. 22.

A good number of commentators make the connection between the seas crossed by the Celts and the 'sea' of the desert.[9] It is possible to die of thirst in both such seas. The physical landscape of islands draws both concepts together. Islands are often remote, unpopulated wildernesses and by definition it is necessary to cross the sea to reach them. Islands represent deserts that are located in the midst of another kind of desert.

The paradox of the desert theme lies in the idea of withdrawal for mission. Withdrawal from the world allowed the monks to wrestle with the forces of evil in such a way that mission would be possible. Despite all of the apparent dissimilarities between the monks in the Egyptian desert and the monks on remote British and Irish islands, this one theme united them in a bond of complete understanding.[10] Whether it was to save the church from worldliness, as in the case of the Middle East, or to expand it by missionary teaching, as with the Celtic church, the forces of darkness had to be overcome and that was only possible through the prayers of those dedicated to a life of holiness. It was to this end that the sacred spaces were dedicated.

Within the holy sites further spaces were identified and marked. The first space was that of the monastic community itself. The wall of the monastery was not designed to shut out the secular. Within the boundaries of the settlement there was a good deal of interaction between sacred and secular. For example, the traditions of the bards were encouraged, as were other artistic and cultural activities. Within the monastery walls, the power of good prevailed. The secular was in that

---

[9] The most thorough exploration of this theme can be found in E. Bowen, *Saints, Seaways and Settlements* (University of Wales Press, 1977).
[10] A good introduction to the desert fathers can be found in James Wellard, *Desert Pilgrimage* (Hutchinson, 1970).

sense made sacred because it was infused with the good. To some extent the monastic community could act as a microcosm for society as a whole. In many cases the monasteries were sufficiently large that they were significant microcosms, capable of modelling the Christian life for a wider society and able to provide dynamic leadership for that society.

Within the sacred space bounded by the walls of the monastery there were other spaces which were especially sacred. In general these were the areas where relics were kept or small churches or chapels were established. The church buildings were almost always small and this reflects the fact that most communities began with only small numbers of monks or nuns, usually no more than ten or twelve people. As monasteries grew, the numbers of churches or chapels grew to accommodate worshippers in groups as compared with the tendency in other traditions to build larger churches so as to accommodate all the worshippers in one building.

Especially sacred places were marked by crosses. These might be areas surrounded by a circle of crosses, or cloister,[11] or they might be marked only by a single cross. The origin of and importance of the Celtic cross will be discussed in a later chapter. But, for now, it is only important to note that they had the function of marking sacred spaces and in doing so delineated what we might call cosmic boundaries.

Marking the Boundaries, Bringing the Good

Philip Sheldrake writes of the importance of boundary places for Celtic Christians.[12] He points out that two kinds of

---

[11] Sheldrake, *Living Between Worlds*, p. 49.
[12] Ibid., p. 29.

boundaries were important. One was the boundary between eternity and the present symbolised by the placing of a cross at a burial site. The physical remains of those who have died allows a reminder of the connectivity between the realities of this world and the next. In this sense, crosses marked 'what might be called cosmic entrance and exit points where the material world and the world of the spirit were believed to come into especially close contact'.[13]

The second relates to the broader notion of boundaries between territories, for example the points at which two kingdoms touch or where two radically different geographical landscapes meet. Of course, sometimes the boundaries between kingdoms are themselves reinforced by physical features of the landscape such as rivers or mountain ranges. A number of Celtic monasteries seem to have been established in such places. The symbolism suggests that the boundary between heaven and earth might be especially thin at these places and also that the existence of a monastic community helps in some way to bind together that which might seem fragmentary or fragile.

The act of being present at the boundaries, on the frontiers, is pregnant with the general Celtic view of the interpenetration of the material world by the spiritual world. These are not two entirely separate realities connected only by death, the one to be feared or ignored. Rather, a proper engagement with the spiritual realm enriches and informs the material world. The God who is good seeks a reconciliation with a world gone astray. The essentially good character of the created order is confirmed and safeguarded by the life of a holy

---

[13] Ibid., pp. 49–50.

community. Through the Christian community the goodness of heaven overspills into the present world bringing peace, harmony and genuine well-being.

The task, then, of the Celtic missionary is to work with God to bring harmony or blessing to the created order and to human community. The life of prayer represents an essential element in that process. As with monastic communities generally, the round of prayer brings a rhythm and hence a harmony to life. The very regularity, consistence and frequency of prayer seeks to establish order in the midst of threatening chaos. There is nothing specifically Celtic about such a practice – it is shared by all who seek a monastic vocation. However, in a Celtic setting, the pattern of praying in the monastic community is extended to a natural interpenetration of prayer with the whole of life. Prayer is seen as lying just below the surface of ordinary human activity and intercourse, ready to be called on and used in a variety of situations. This kind of prayer is both healing and life-giving.

One writer records the charge made at the Council of Macon in 627 to the effect that the disciples of Columbanus made 'the sign of the cross too frequently on things of daily use and for uttering too many benedictions on entering and quitting places'.[14] The benedictions referred to may well have been the frequent Celtic prayers of blessing. Places, occasions, actions and people could all be the subject of prayers of blessing. Prayers of blessing could be said in relation to the action of sleep, children might receive a blessing, the day could be blessed, as could homes, doorways and utensils. The

---

[14] Agrestius, from Jonas' *Vita Columba*, II, 9; also cited in L. Gougaud, *Christianity in Celtic Lands* (Sheed & Ward, 1922), pp. 337–8.

deliberations of those who might give judgements could be blessed. There was no codification of appropriate blessings so much as a feeling that prayers of blessing might easily spill out from a sense of gratitude for the whole of life. There was an awareness that God was over all and in all.

The sovereign power of God was expressed in frequent prayers of blessing that sought his protection. Once again, the situation and occasions for which protection might be sought were very diverse. Undoubtedly the best-known such prayer is 'St Patrick's Breastplate', of which the following is an extract:

> May Christ protect me today
> against poison and burning,
> against drowning and wounding,
> so that I may have abundant reward;
> Christ with me, Christ before me, Christ behind me;
> Christ within me, Christ beneath me, Christ above me;
> Christ to right of me, Christ to left of me;
> Christ in my lying, Christ in my sitting, Christ in my
>   rising;
> Christ in the heart of all who think of me,
> Christ on the tongue of all who speak to me,
> Christ in the eye of all who see me,
> Christ in the ear of all who hear me.[15]

The form of St Patrick's Breastplate is echoed in many other prayers of protection. Prayers for daily protection were common as were prayers at the start or end of journeys. The intent

---

[15] This, along with many other passages from original Celtic sources, can be found in Oliver Davies and Fiona Bowie, *Celtic Christian Spirituality* (SPCK, 1995).

to invoke protection speaks both of an awareness of the power of God and of an understanding of the nature of the malign forces against which protection was required. It was not merely a question of seeking protection for the ordinary human processes of life. For example, the practice of 'saining' or blessing to ensure that no evil spirits were present was also common. The story is told of an occasion when Columba blessed a pail of milk brought to him by a young monk. After he blessed it, the milk was disturbed by a demon and half the milk was spilt. The monk had forgotten to 'sain' the pail before milking!

The point of the story is not so much to induce anxiety over the presence of demons in the everyday aspects of life as to demonstrate the need to bring goodness, routinely to cast out evil so that good is extended into every corner of existence. The one who protects also brings blessing. The state of being blessed is one of peace, contentment, at-one-ness, the *shalom* or well-being of the Old Testament reflected also in the Beatitudes.

To seek to bring good is also to recognise that which is good in all things. Such a view implies a very particular approach to mission. The Whitby debates and the Celtic disappointment at the conclusion had little to do with dismay at the loss of an intellectual argument, still less any worry over a loss of power. It was far more a recognition that something had been lost at a much deeper level. While conversion in the Roman tradition seemed to mean conforming to an orderliness based on ecclesial authority, for the Celts, conversion was much more a heart response to the love of God as seen in the whole of creation. Wisdom more than canon law is what really mattered to the Celtic Christians. Celtic spirituality was able to take that which was good in the cultures encountered and build on it as Christ was revealed to the pagans. The stories found in the Bible could be recounted as a means of sharing wisdom with those who had discovered some truth and who sought more.

6

WINNING HEARTS,
WINNING MINDS

As we have already seen, the position of the druids was critical in Celtic society. Despite their prohibition on the writing down of knowledge, and hence the absence of books, the druids must be seen as both the holders of wisdom and learning as well as the guardians of religious rituals. They were, in effect, all the learned professions rolled into one: priest, solicitor, scientist and poet. As Pomponius Mela, a contemporary of St Paul noted, 'they profess to know the size and shape of the world, the movements of the heavens and the stars, and the will of the gods'.[1] The arrival of Christian missions in the form of the Celtic saints not only challenged the role of the druids in the specifically religious sphere, the scholarship of the Celtic saints allowed them also to assume the more general role of men of learning. Mission was not just to hearts but also to minds.

Although it may seem obvious to us that there is an association between the monastery and learning, such a connection

---

[1] See John McNeill, *The Celtic Churches: A History* AD *200 to 1200* (University of Chicago Press, 1974), pp. 8–9.

was not there of necessity. Indeed, the earliest monasteries in the east made no such connection. It was only the form of monasticism pioneered in the west by St Martin, and adopted by the earliest Celtic saints, that introduced a more scholarly emphasis than that found in the Egyptian desert.[2] It is therefore important to try and understand why this difference occurred. To some extent this development can be understood in terms of context. The Egyptian hermit was attempting to escape a worldly church and so was hardly likely to take a library with him in his search for simplicity. The monasticism of the west however was rather different. There was a clear missionary intent dedicated to the winning of souls. The period covered by the mature ministry of Martin of Tours was identical to that of the most critical expansion of the church province of Gaul. This was an intentionally missionary church and large numbers of influential families became Christians during this time.

ESTABLISHING THE TRADITION

Unlike the Egyptian monasteries, the location of St Martin's monastery, near his episcopal seat, was not a hindrance to the creation of a resource for learning. More significantly, the bishops of Gaul, beginning with Irenaeus of Lyons, had developed something of a tradition in countering the various heresies that plagued the church from time to time. These men were scholars who were familiar with the best thought of their day. The possibility of a scholarly resource was bound to be

---

[2] A clear view of the origins of Western monasticism can be found in Joseph Lienhard, *Paulinus of Nola and Early Western Monasticism* (Hanstein, 1977).

attractive for those engaged in such a task. The monastery, which had attracted able and literate recruits, was a natural agency for this purpose. Clearly, even apart from the fertile possibilities suggested by the context in which St Martin worked, such a development would hardly have been possible apart from the orientation of Martin himself. He was a scholar of some renown and part of the appeal of living near him, of seeing him as a mentor, was to benefit from his teaching as well as his spiritual example.

The pioneering initiative of Martin of Tours was further reinforced by two other notable monasteries in Gaul, both of which developed a scholarly tradition. John Cassian established a community near Marseilles.[3] John was famous for his authorship of two books, *De Institutis Coenobiorum* and the *Collationes*. St Honoratus founded a monastery at Lerins, a group of islands off the Riviera. Honoratus had been trained in Greece and he brought the learning of a classical tradition to his community. Lerins was famed for providing Gaul with many of its later leaders and a good many British and Irish Celts were thought to have studied at some time or another within its walls. It is suggested that even St Patrick studied there.

The flavour of Martin's learning was taken by Ninian to Candida Casa, which in turn influenced monastic communities in Wales and Ireland. Some foundations in Wales were directly influenced by the work of Martin. This tradition was continued in the crucial development of the Irish monasteries and was continued by those who were sent to Scotland,

---

[3] See Owen Chadwick, *John Cassian: A Study in Primitive Monasticism* (CUP, 1950).

England and the continent of Europe. The most prominent
of all the Irish missionaries on the mainland of Europe, St
Columbanus, was recognised as one of the leading scholars of
his day. On the basis of his learning, Columbanus was ready to
dispute with Pope Gregory himself.

This love of learning was not the prerogative of the few. It
is clear that many of the Celtic saints had a great love for learning and books as a missionary resource. Leslie Hardinge writes:

> A legend is told of Cummine, who was once asked what
> he would most like in his church. 'I should like it full of
> books,' he said, 'for them to go to students, and to sow
> God's word in the ears of every one, [so as] to bring him
> to heaven out of the track of the Devil.' In the Lives
> books are often associated with the saints. On the day of
> his death Columba was depicted as transcribing a book.[4]

From the earliest days of Celtic Christianity, holy men and
women have been inextricably connected with the role of
scholar. One of the earliest and most famous of Celtic scholars
was Illtud, whose monastery at Llantwit Major was founded in
the latter part of the fifth century, and enjoyed a glowing reputation as a centre of learning. It is said that Illtud drew David,
Samson, Gildas and Paulinus, amongst others, through his
reputation.[5] The position of the man of learning (later to be
known in Ireland as the *fer leginn*) was firmly in place at this
earliest stage and carried on by many others. Even those who

---

[4] Leslie Hardinge, *The Celtic Church in Britain* (SPCK, 1972), p. 191.
[5] See Elissa Henken, *Traditions of the Welsh Saints* (D. S. Brewer, 1987), for
the stories of these saints and many others.

were famed more for their lives on the continent, such as Columbanus, learnt their linguistic and exegetical skills while still in their Irish, Welsh and British schools of learning.

The later flowering of this scholarly tradition can be seen in the enormous impact made by the two Irish scholars living in the ninth century. A number of Irishmen visited the court of Charles the Bald in Liege, apparently bringing greetings from the Irish king of the day. These Irishmen were on pilgrimage to Rome. One particular Irishman, Sedulius Scotus, made an impact on the court. It is not clear whether he came with the other Irish party or whether his presence at the same time was entirely coincidental. He was known as a poet, scholar, scribe, courtier and theologian. His writings reveal that he was well acquainted with the classical writers as well as being thoroughly familiar with the scholarship of his day. A number of scholars have suggested that the sophistication of his Latin style indicated a considerable ability. In keeping with the illusive qualities of the Irish *peregrini*, it is said that 'Like some uncharted comet the Irishman Sedulius appeared at Liège about the middle of the ninth century (845–58) to vanish again as mysteriously as he had come.'[6]

The second Irishman to make an impact on the ninth-century world of Charles the Bald, was the noted scholar, Johannes Scotus Eriugena (which should be translated as John the Irishman).[7] John was centred at Laon and Rheims. He

---

[6] M. Laistner, *Thought and Letters in Western Europe* (London, 1957), p. 251; cited in Myles Dillon, and Nora Chadwick, *The Celtic Realms* (Weidenfeld & Nicolson, 1967).

[7] For an academic, yet readable, account of Eriugena see Dermot Moran, *The Philosophy of John Scotus Eriugena: A Study of Idealism in the Middle Ages* (CUP, 1989).

knew both Greek and Latin and although it is unlikely that he was a priest and may not have had a mission in mind in the way that Columbanus had in earlier times, the brilliance of his mind demonstrated the riches of the Irish tradition begun so many years earlier, which made a steady and significant contribution to the enrichment of European thought and civilisation.

TAKING THE HIGH GROUND

The development of a scholarly tradition amongst the monasteries of Ireland was not merely the inevitable consequence of the inheritance of St Martin. While it is certainly true that scholarship can be valued for its own sake, there were also sound missiological reasons for its continuance within the context of Ireland and subsequently elsewhere.

The priority of mission acted as a critical catalyst for the pursuit of study. Clearly, a degree of learning gave an impetus to the spread of the faith in that it encouraged kings and other members of the nobility to send their children to monasteries in order to receive a good education. But beyond this pragmatic consideration, the task of evangelisation faced by the Irish saints greatly benefited from a scholarly tradition. They were concerned to influence a whole culture and not just to win individuals to the faith. Of course, the issues are strongly related. Well-educated individuals who came to faith in the context of the monastery were helpful in producing change in Ireland. But the issue goes beyond such an outcome. Although it is true that the Irish saints did not face a literate Celtic culture, they nevertheless were dealing with a people who had a strong oral culture which had its own ideas of learning.

The Celtic saints needed to be able to offer an alternative interpretation of Celtic tradition and not merely to see individual converts attach their new faith to an essentially pagan tradition. This required an intellectual rigour and discipline. In the view of the Irish saints, the light of the gospel needed to penetrate the culture at a deeper level. It was not enough merely to produce individuals with a personal morality based on the inspiration of Christ, helpful as this might be to the individual concerned. The transfer of Celtic culture from an oral to a written code was not just an incidental or even inevitable and natural process. Celtic tradition held that religious knowledge, ancient wisdom and even the law itself should not be written down – it must be entrusted only to those who could remember it by virtue of devoting their whole lives to the task. In one sense, given the absence of multiple copies of a book by means of printing, or even the absence of safe structures in which to keep books, keeping knowledge within the body of memory of a guild might actually be safer than entrusting knowledge to a single book that might either by changed, damaged, destroyed or lost.

The library was usually an urban phenomenon.[8] At the very least a library relied on the existence of a large and prosperous villa. Handwritten books were, after all, an expensive luxury. Celtic society in Ireland was rural and, while the Romano-British culture preserved some aspects of an urban culture, the departure of the Romans and the arrival of the Angles and Saxons largely ended this structure. As we have already suggested, in Wales it is possible that the first monasteries were based on former villas, while in Ireland the creation

---

[8] McNeill, *The Celtic Churches*, p. 123, and Philip Sheldrake, *Living Between Worlds* (DLT, 1995), p. 40.

of large monasteries became the closest structure that Irish society had to towns and thus to an urban society. In this sense the monasteries offered the first real possibility of a structure within which a literate community could be created. Not only could books be kept in safety in such a place but there was also a means of copying books to safeguard their contents further.

One writer describes the care with which the books were kept:

> Each scriptorium had its own library. The books were kept in satchels, and hung from the rafters in the scribe's hut. The satchels were of leather, and tooled and decorated. The more valuable the book the more elaborate was the case in which it was stored. Sometimes the container was made of metal, and embellished with precious stones. The library of Bobbio, at the end of the tenth century, contained no fewer than seven hundred volumes.[9]

The monastic communities modelled themselves on the Old Testament city and began to rework Celtic law and society using the Old Testament scriptures as a starting point for a codification of the law. According to tradition, Patrick direct-ed a revision of the brehon code of Ireland. The Decalogue, which was a key inspiration for this revision, together with the Psalms played an important part in the worship of the Celtic church. The Senchus Mor (see glossary) points to the nature of this process in two ways. First, it suggests that the Old Testament was consistent with Irish culture and did not seek to

---

[9] Hardinge, *The Celtic Church in Britain*, p. 194.

revoke the existing structure entirely, 'for the law of nature had prevailed where the written law did not reach'.[10]

Second, it makes clear that the principle employed by the Celtic missionaries was to preserve all that did not actually clash with the Word of God. That which was added to the brehon code by the monks mostly related to the relationship between church and society, 'for the law of nature had been quite right, except the faith, and its obligations and the harmony of the church and the people. And this is the Senchus Mor.'[11]

Therefore, we see that the process of missionary contextualisation was not different in principle from that attempted by the church in the Mediterranean as it sought to adapt a Jewish church to the needs of a Hellenistic culture. However, the means used were rather different. One possible reason for this difference lies in the nature of the perceived obstacles to the faith. The church of the first few centuries used a great deal of its energies to explain the faith in the context of the philosophical tradition that occupied the intellectual high ground. The key obstacle for the Celtic saints was not a well-formed intellectual philosophical system so much as an active religious paganism which drew on well-formed traditions and wisdom. The use of scripture was a key ingredient in their approach. That raises the question as to how the Celts used scripture in their mission.

[10] Ibid., p. 49.
[11] Ibid.

BIBLICAL THEOLOGY

The Celts did read non-biblical texts. The Celtic saints had
access to numerous pagan and classical authors, Virgil being
a favourite text. There are seventh-century glosses on both
Bucolics and *Georgics*.[12] Because of their pagan origins these
texts were reserved for those with unshakeable faith. Young
novices were not permitted to read them. Even when the
monks were reading commentaries by the church fathers such
as Origen, Jerome and Hilary, they were only ever used as a
tool in the greater understanding of the scriptures themselves:
they were not thought to have any real 'intrinsic value' of their
own. All the reading and linguistic study undertaken by the
Celtic monks had one goal and one goal only: the study of the
Bible. It is this clear path that drew so many famous and noble
contemporaries to their monastery gates.

The Celts were interested in etymology.[13] They carefully
studied the meaning of key words in the Bible. It seems that
they gained such knowledge from the explanation of a number
of commentators to whom they seemed to have had access.
However, although they may have known the original Greek
or Hebrew meaning of the words they studied, there is little
evidence that knowledge of Greek and Hebrew was widespread
in the monasteries or that they were taught as separate disciplines. Latin was certainly known and it would have been
impossible to have studied the Bible without a working knowledge of that language if only because the Bible which was the

---

[12] Two significant Latin works by Virgil.
[13] For a full account of learning methods employed within the Irish
monastery see Kathleen Hughes, *Early Christian Ireland: Introduction to the
Sources* (Hodder & Stoughton, 1972), ch. 6.

most popular with Celtic Christians was the Old Latin, called the Itala. Later, when the Celts were more fully Romanised, the Vulgate replaced the Itala.

The key method of the Celts was to allow a knowledge of scripture to permeate their thinking at every level. The Bible was used exclusively as a means of appeal. Biblical citations appear frequently in those writings of the Celtic saints that have been preserved. The various lives of the saints emphasise the degree to which they were well acquainted with the scriptures. This was a noted feature of their ministry. Such a testimony was no mere hagiography, as it is borne out by the written evidence that is available. For example, the writings of St Patrick are full of biblical quotations.[14] In the *Confession* and in the 'Letter to Coroticus', one scholar has noted 340 examples from 46 books of the Bible. Patrick's usage of scripture is very typical of the way in which scripture was looked to as an authority by the Celts. In exactly the same way Gildas the Briton also used the Bible as a sole reference point from which to derive authority for his various arguments.

The exclusive appeal to scripture carries with it certain implications concerning the authority which the Celts accorded to the various councils of the Church in particular, and to

---

[14] Patrick's 'Hymn of Secundus' gives a glimpse of his reliance on the Bible for his theology:

He finds in the sacred volume the sacred treasure …
Whose words are seasoned with the divine oracles …
Whose seeds are seen to be the Gospel of Christ …
He sings Hymns with the Apocalypse, and the Psalms of God,
On which also he discourses, for the edification of the people of God;
Which scripture he believes, in the trinity of the sacred name,
And teaches the One substance in Three persons.

church tradition in general. Various church leaders from the Celtic churches had attended some of the Western councils. This meant that they were clearly aware of the decisions of the councils. Moreover, they also knew a good deal about various church traditions beyond their own, but they did not appeal either to the decisions of the councils or to church tradition as authoritative. The decisions of the councils and the wisdom of tradition could be used as confirmation of a scripture but not the other way round. For example, Columbanus referred to tradition in justifying the distinct practices of the Celts, but this is not the same as referring to tradition as a unique authority on a par with the scriptures.

The Bible, then, was authoritative over and against any other document or tradition. It contained the words of life. Confidence in the value of its revelation allowed the Celts to see it as an ultimate source of authority, not just for individual believers in the area of morality, nor merely for the church in the sphere of doctrine, important as these might be, but as a means of addressing the fundamental order of society.

A number of writers describe this approach as comprising a Biblical Theology. But what does such a concept really mean? A number of elements were important. First, the canon of scripture was seen as a unity. For the Celts the whole of scripture was important and no part was seen as somehow less than scripture.

Second, the Old Testament had to be interpreted in the light of the New Testament. For very practical reasons, the Celts in Ireland used elements of the Old Testament law in order to regulate society. But just as the law of Moses had replaced an earlier set of customs in the Semitic world that were somewhat arbitrary in their cruelty, so the Old Testament laws used by the Celts replaced penalties that were significantly more severe. The light of the New Testament and the kindness of Christ were allowed to permeate Old Testament requirements.

Third, the scriptures were understood from the perspective of the Trinity. The doctrine of the Trinity was vitally important to the Celts. It is difficult to know exactly where this fondness for a Trinitarian formula comes from. Certainly Irenaeus, the intellectual forbear of the Celts, was passionate in his defence of an essentially Trinitarian doctrine, though of course a fully worked Trinitarian theology was not formed until later. It was also true that the notion of a triadic pattern could be found deep in pagan Celtic thought and it is possible that this was a helpful concept to employ in explaining the Christian notion of the Godhead.[15] That the pagans had already understood the triadic nature underlying reality would not have troubled the Celtic saints since they carried the conviction that the natural law had already revealed some truths which could only be fully understood in the light of the gospel itself.

Fourth, the application of scripture was intensely practical. Behaviour in accordance with the gospels eclipsed the old Irish and Welsh pagan laws; the study of scripture was the foundation for the increase of reading and writing and the inspiration for new generations of creativity.[16] The Celtic commentator was concerned to apply the Bible to life situations.

Fifth, the approach of the Celt to the Bible was rather literalistic, in that the simple meaning of the Bible was accepted

---

[15] See Miranda Green, *The Gods of the Celts* (Alan Salton, 1986), with special reference to her comments on the 'triple mothers', a fertility symbol which relied on a tripart.

[16] Hardinge, *The Celtic Church in Britain*, pp. 29–30.

without too much stress being placed on its allegorical or symbolic significance. Leslie Hardinge notes that:

> On the Psalmist's reference to the quote 'enemies' the comment was, 'These are the Moabites, Ammonites, and Idumeans.' The commentator read Psalm 108 and applied it to the days of Hezekiah, noting that the 'fool' quote referred to Sennacherib. St Paul's prediction of the 'falling away', was taken to refer to the departure of the Empire from the Romans.[17]

The methods of interpretation used by the Celts are known to us through a study of a number of manuscripts which offer a record of Celtic exposition of the scriptures. As one might expect from those who took the authority of scripture seriously, the most important means of understanding scripture was to look to its historical and literal meaning. It was recognised that this historic application might have a more general meaning which could be applied to the present condition of the expositor and his audience.

Leslie Hardinge suggests that occasionally a threefold (and sometimes a fourfold), system of interpretation was used. The three would be the literal meaning (*stoir*), the mystical or allegorical meaning (*sens*) which related to its eternal significance, and the moral meaning (*morolus*) which had to do with its present practical meaning.[18] The underlying suggestion in such an approach is that the commentator does not wish to

---

[17] Ibid., pp. 37–8.
[18] Ibid., p. 38. There were, however, many ways of interpreting the Bible, as any early period of biblical studies manifests, such as the numerous systems developed within the Patristic period.

move too far from the actual text in order to engage in the kind of elaborate speculation that was sometimes to be found in the works of some Eastern fathers, such as Origen.[19] It also illustrates an approach to the scriptures which sees other sources, such as the Apocrypha, the fathers and the church councils as useful only when they confirm the existing conclusion of the commentator and not as authoritative in their own right. The transmission of knowledge of the scriptures accompanied by careful teaching of their meaning was therefore a significant element in the missionary practice of the Celts.

PREACHING THE WORD

Preaching was a primary method employed by the Celtic saints in their missionary enterprise. It is evident from Bede's writings that some of the Saints were renowned for their preaching skills. Bede writes of Cuthbert:

> In those days, whenever a clerk or priest visited a town, English folk always used to gather at his call to hear the Word, eager to hear his message and even more eager to carry out whatever they had heard and understood. But Cuthbert was so skilful a speaker, and had such a light in his angelic face, and such a love for proclaiming his message, that none presumed to hide his inmost secrets, but all openly confessed their wrong-doing; for they felt it impossible to conceal their guilt from him, and at his direction they blotted out by works of

---

[19] For a good discussion of Origen see H. Crouzel, *Origen* (Paris, 1989), and A. Trigg, *Origen* (SCM Press, 1985).

penance the sins that they had confessed. He used mainly to visit and preach in the villages that lay far distant among high and inaccessible mountains, which others feared to visit and whose barbarity and squalor daunted other teachers. Cuthbert, however, gladly undertook this pious task, and taught with such patience and skill that when he left the monastery it would sometimes be for a week, sometimes two or three, and occasionally an entire month, before he returned home, after staying in the mountains to guide the peasants heavenward by his teachings and virtuous example.[20]

A number of sources give us some idea of what this Celtic preaching was like. The Old-Irish glosses contain thousands of notes which seem to be the views or thoughts of the preachers as they prepared to speak to their congregations. One Irish source gives the detailed views of a teacher who advises his students on sermon preparation. In addition, there are a few Old-Irish homilies which have survived intact and these have been analysed by scholars. It is clear from all of these sources that scripture was lovingly and frequently quoted, usually in its original Old Latin form and then paraphrased in Old Irish for the benefit of the congregation. Extempore preaching was a common feature as the practical application of the passages were explored. Simplicity, imagination and practicality in terms of everyday life surround their exposition of the scripture.

---

[20] Bede, *A History of the English Church and People* (Penguin, 1988), IV, 27.

THE CLEANSING OF THE MIND

But if the practical intent of preaching from the Bible was to produce everyday application of the scriptures, the missionary intent lay deeper than the conversion of pagans and the maturation of believers. There was a view that the recitation of the scripture cleansed the mind and the spirit from a pagan past. Leslie Hardinge illustrates this view in the following passage:

> In a conversation which Germanus had with his friend the Abbot Nestorus, Germanus inquired as to the best way of expelling from the mind the notions of pagan authors. The Abbot replied in effect: 'Read the sacred books with the same zeal that you read heathen writers and your thoughts will be pure.' And so the pious Christian bent his energies to mastering the Bible. Cassian set aside the commentators and advised his disciples to do the same, devoting their time to prayer, fasting, and meditation, so as to reach an understanding of the Scriptures, promising that God would reveal to them in their dreams the sense of the passages which they thus considered.[21]

The notion of soaking the mind in scripture so as to produce a purity of thought was not an appeal to scripture as magic. Rather, the intent was to produce minds which thought biblically, were inspired by biblical images, and informed by biblical values. This practice, begun early by those such as Cassian, seems to have been widespread by the time of Aidan. Bede

---

[21] Hardinge, *The Celtic Church in Britain*, p. 33.

writes of him: 'His life is in marked contrast to the apathy of our own times, for all who walked with him, whether monks or layfolk, were required to meditate, that is, either to read the Scriptures or to learn the Psalms. This was their daily occupation wherever they went ...'[22]

The monastic communities developed lives which were shaped around prayer and study of the scriptures. Even the copying of the scriptures, so that others might have access to their words, was thought to have a beneficial effect on the minds of those who did the copying. The Bible acted as a foundation for the communal life, for the individual's spiritual life and as a means of reforming the wider society around laws that were pleasing to God. To encourage biblical thinking was to complete the missionary task of bringing individuals and a whole culture under the reign of Christ.

[22] Bede, *History*, III, 5.

7

THE CATHEDRAL OF CREATION:
MISSION AND THE COSMOS

 To learn to think rightly, with Christ at the centre of our thoughts, is also to rethink the way in which we relate to others and so to the natural world around us. The cleansing word of the scriptures acts to re-enchant the natural world. Thinking biblically means that our fellow humankind cannot be regarded as simply those who meet our needs. In the same way we cannot view the natural world as an ordinary thing to be exploited for our benefit. Thinking biblically about the world helps to re-enchant a habitat stripped of mystical content. To think biblically is to see even the obviously material, wealth itself, as also potentially a sacrament.[1]

It might be a surprise for some to think that Christians could view nature as essentially sacred – reflecting the presence and purpose of God. It is true that the contemporary interest in the natural world, so powerfully represented by what we have come to know as the Green Movement, has been embraced by Christians just as enthusiastically as by those with no particular religious commitment. Yet Christians

---

[1] J. Ellul, *Money and Power* (Marshall Pickering, 1986), pp. 62–3.

sometimes find themselves reeling in surprise at the virulent
blame that is attached to the Christian tradition by some apologists amongst the Greens who identify Christianity as a
primary cause of humankind's assault on the natural world.
Christianity has often been seen as the enemy of all things
Green.

The writer Ian Bradley traces the origins of this attitude
to a formative article published in the American magazine
Science in 1967.[2] The author of that article, Professor Lynn
White, suggested that the animism present in pagan religions
was overthrown by a Christianity solely concerned with the
needs of people. White argued that a totally human-centred
approach to life, which he associates with Christianity, deni-
grates nature to the status of a supplier of the needs of
humankind.

It is not difficult to argue that such a view represents a
complete distortion of the message of Christianity. Ian Bradley,
amongst others, provides a powerful apologetic which clearly
indicates why Christianity should not be seen as a villain by
those with Green sympathies. But the very fact that the case
has been made at all provides some food for thought. Whether
we care to admit it or not, the recent history of the Western
world has produced a degree of alienation between humanity
and the natural world. Many of us feel this sense of alienation
even when we are unable to understand why this should be.
Further, we have to acknowledge that the forces which have
produced such a sense of crisis have come into being in the
context of the nominally Christian West. Science and technology have been the instruments of a changed relationship

---

[2] Ian Bradley, *God is Green* (DLT, 1990), p. 1.

with the world, sometimes for good but also for ill. Many have noted that science and technology are the legitimate children of Christianity. Christians would tend to respond that the deception represented by the myths of secularism has caused these disciplines to become wayward children.[3]

For those who are grappling with a sense of alienation from nature, the witness of the Celtic saints comes as a refreshing breeze. Although it was undoubtedly true that the Celtic monastic communities sought to create sacred spaces,[4] this was not because they thought that the rest of the world was intrinsically evil. Their concern was not so much to shut out the world as to recover its essentially sacred character.

In a very powerful sense, the Celtic saints recognised that the paganism they faced did not necessarily see the created order as holy. While the pre-Christian paganism of the Celts certainly understood the essential underlying unity of nature and clearly saw the influence of the spiritual in creation, that was a long way from seeing nature as holy or sacred. The pre-Christian notion of the sacred nature of certain groves or rivers is undoubtedly attractive to those who aspire to a Green theology. But those who wish to espouse such a romantic view of our pagan past need also to face the reality of pagan human sacrifice, a practice decidedly unattractive yet no less real.

The pagan idea that each tree, brook, well or even certain stones were inhabited by their own spirit was an essentially ambiguous claim. It left open to question whether the spirit of each object was friendly or malign. Pagan religion seeks to propitiate such spirits – at best to live in harmony with them – but

---

[3] For a fuller discussion of these issues see Martin Robinson, *The Faith of the Unbeliever* (Monarch, 1994).

[4] See Philip Sheldrake, *Living Between Worlds* (DLT, 1995), chs. 2, 3.

the element of fear is certainly present. For the Celtic saints the natural elements were expressions of the good God who had created them. The created order was not ambiguous: it was intrinsically good and intended for the good of humankind.

This fundamental conviction is graphically represented by the frequent stories attached to the saints of their fondness for the natural world. One story attached to Modomnoc, a disciple of St David, tells of how he had been responsible for keeping the bees in the monastery at Mynyw. When the time came for Modomnoc to return to Ireland, the bees came with him to his ship. According to the story, he returned them three times before David blessed the bees and instructed him to take the bees with him. The story continues by suggesting that the bees did go with him and then prospered in a land where bees had never previously been able to thrive.[5]

A good many stories suggest that the saints had powers that caused wild animals to minister to the needs of the saints. The legends suggest that the saints also had power on occasion to tame wild animals.[6] These stories, as with the story of Patrick's banishment of snakes from Ireland, suggest a link between holiness, the overcoming of evil and the reharmonization of nature. The reconciliatory power of the gospel extends beyond the realm of the human and into the natural order.

Nor is it merely animals that respond to the ministrations of the saints. Columba is said to have calmed the sea, Beuno is said to have caused miraculous trees to grow, while numerous saints are said to have caused certain streams or wells to have

---

[5] Elissa Henken, *Traditions of the Welsh Saints* (D. S. Brewer, 1987), p. 63.
[6] Cuthbert, more than anyone, was known to have close friendships with animals. The best place to read about these is in Bede's *Life of Cuthbert*, in *The Age of Bede*, trans. J.F. Webb, ed. D.H. Farmer (Penguin, 1965).

healing properties. The natural world also features at the time of the birth of certain of the saints. Signs that appear in the created order point to the special significance or potential holiness of the one who is being born. Even where a well or stream had previously been thought to have held healing properties, the linkage with the healing power of Christ sets that healing character firmly within the context of the broader salvation represented by the gospel message.

This interconnectedness between the Celtic saints and the natural world is reflected in the poetry that flows from this same tradition:

> Almighty Creator, it is you who have made the land
> and the sea ...
> The world cannot comprehend in song bright and
> melodious,
> even though the grass and the trees should sing,
> all your wonders, O true Lord!
> The Father created the world by a miracle;
> it is difficult to express its measure.
> Letters cannot contain it, letters cannot comprehend it.
> Jesus created for the hosts of Christendom,
> with miracles when he came,
> resurrection through his nature.
>
> He who made the wonder of the world,
> will save us, has saved us.
> It is not too great a toil to praise the Trinity.[7]

---

[7] An old Welsh poem, c. ninth century, cited in Oliver Davies and Fiona Bowie, *Celtic Christian Spirituality* (SPCK, 1995), p. 27.

Clearly, the identification of holiness and an affinity with nature, and the connection between salvation for humanity accompanying wonder at the created order, is not entirely unique to the Celtic tradition. Much the same theme can be found in the broader Western Catholic tradition as represented by saints such as St Francis. But the emphasis on such an identity with the natural world does stand in contrast with the various accounts of the Roman contemporaries of the Celts. The accounts of the work of the Roman-based missions do not place the same emphasis on their relationship with the natural order. We cannot say that the various Roman saints did not have an affinity for nature, but there does seem to be a difference of emphasis. That Celtic difference of emphasis is not accidental, but flows from a theological perspective that stands in marked contrast with a Roman understanding. In particular, it flows from the very positive view that the Celts held of the way in which God works in his created order, including an assessment of human nature itself. We can gain some sense of how this difference reveals itself by looking more closely at the contentious views of the British theologian Pelagius.

THE IMPACT OF SIN ON THE CREATED ORDER[8]

Although we do not know the early details of the life of Pelagius, we know that he was a Christian at precisely the time that Martin of Tours was beginning to exercise an influence on

---

[8] Many accounts of the Pelagian controversy can be found; one of the better ones, which really uncovers who Pelagius actually was, as well as Augustine's interpretation of the controversy, is B. Rees, *Pelagius: A Reluctant Heretic* (The Boydell Press, 1988).

the Celtic church throughout Gaul and in parts of the British Isles. It is likely that Pelagius was influenced by this ascetic brand of Christianity. Some believe he was originally an Irish monk who had settled in southern Wales prior to his journey to the European mainland. In any case, we can be certain that he arrived in Rome sometime in the last years of the fourth century.[9] This dating places Pelagius as a contemporary of St Martin and would have allowed him contact with that early form of Celtic Christianity which was to flower in the monastic life of those such as St Illtud whose ministry began shortly after the death of Pelagius. It was during his preaching ministry in Rome that Pelagius first came to the attention of the wider Christian world.

While in Rome, Pelagius began to direct his preaching against what he felt were the lax conditions prevailing amongst the Christians of that city. In this regard Pelagius was entirely consistent with his much later Celtic compatriot, Columbanus. His was a call for holiness, and in particular for the notion that it was incumbent upon Christians to strive for perfection. In itself, this idea would have been entirely familiar to those who, like Martin, were attempting to live a life of desert simplicity amongst the temptations present in the urban centres of the Roman Empire. The particular way in which Pelagius sought to express his concerns focused on the question of human free will. It seemed to Pelagius that the way in which the doctrine of grace was being used offered an excuse to Christians to abandon any concern for the way of holiness. It was almost as if Christians were not fully accepting their personal responsibility for action, so certain were they

---

[9] J.W.C. Wand, *A History of the Early Church to* AD *500* (Routledge, 1975), p. 230.

that sin had robbed them of any ability to strive for holiness. Pelagius rejected the idea that the whole of humanity should be viewed as utterly depraved with no capacity for good.

It is clear that there was a good deal of sympathy for the preaching of Pelagius. Not only did he win the support of Rufinus,[10] an important leader within the Christian community of Rome, but much later, when Pelagian views were being suppressed through the action of the emperor, nineteen Italian bishops refused to sign the condemnation of Pelagius which was being used to justify his exile. Significantly, even more substantial support for a Pelagian perspective was to be found in the Eastern church, partly, it is true, amongst the Nestorian Christians, but there was also a broader sympathy for his views amongst the wider Christian community in the East.

Given this degree of support, why was there a problem at all and what was the importance of that problem for the broader Celtic tradition which Pelagius typifies to a significant degree? There may never have been any contention over the views of Pelagius but for the curious coincidence that Pelagius was forced to leave Rome as a result of the sack of that city by Alaric either in the year 409 or 410. He travelled to North Africa and in particular to Carthage which was really a Roman colony rather than an African city. Here he came into immediate conflict with Augustine who had by then developed a doctrine of grace which was potentially in radical disagreement with the view of Pelagius.

It is in this partially accidental and exaggerated conflict that we see some of the hidden differences of emphasis between the later Celtic and Roman missionaries. First, it

---

[10] See Rees, *Pelagius: A Reluctant Heretic*, p. 9.

should be made clear that there was no necessity for a conflict between Pelagius and Augustine. Most scholars are clear that the views of Pelagius became more contentious in the hands of his followers, particularly his disciple Celestius, than Pelagius himself might have wished. Second, we face the additional difficulty that we know more of the views of Pelagius through Augustine's refutation of them than we do from Pelagius directly. Some certainly take the view that Augustine's representation of Pelagius' views are actually a distortion which reflects the positions of his more irascible disciples rather than the man himself. Nevertheless, the outcome of this dispute was that Celestius was condemned at Carthage in 412, again in 416 and finally at the great African council held in Carthage in 418. The already mentioned political pressure and exile further isolated Pelagius a few years before his death and his views were finally anathematised at the council of Ephesus in 431.

But despite this unhappy turn of events, it is abundantly clear that Pelagius' views found considerable continuing sympathy amongst other Christians. The significance of the view of the church in the East lay in the fact that an Eastern view of grace was more strongly connected with the work of the Holy Spirit than with the problems of morality that exercised Augustine. In a similar fashion, the Eastern church resisted the idea that the created order, including the nature of humankind, was entirely corrupted as a result of the Fall. For the church in the East, the image of God as found in creation could never be extinguished by the evil of the Fall. The Celts, with their fondness for the spirituality of the East, and especially their affinity with the work of the Spirit, were much more likely to be drawn to a positive assessment of creation.

This affirmation of the continuing work of God in human nature and in the created order underlies the tendencies found

in the approach of Pelagius. It is therefore no surprise to find
that Pelagian views found some favour amongst some of the
Celtic communities of the West. The writings of Cassian and
then later of Vincent of Lerins, both of whom were influential
in shaping the thought of the later Celts of Britain and Ireland
have been characterised as Semi-Pelagian in character.[11]
Despite the formal refutation of Pelagian doctrines in Britain
as a consequence of the campaigns against Pelagianism by
Germanus and Lupus in the year 429, there remained a difference of emphasis between the more optimistic embrace of
creation by the Celts and the rather more pessimistic suspicion
of nature as represented by the Roman missions, influenced
as they were by the dominant Augustinian tradition of the
Western Catholic church. As one writer has expressed it:

> The real mischief of Augustine's distorted vision and
> its too-ready acceptance at Rome was that he succeed-
> ed in removing the Church's gaze from the Blessed
> Creation, which God created good and which is the
> transfigured image of its Creator. Henceforth it would
> be fixed instead upon Adam's Fall and the doctrine of
> Original Sin.[12]

CREATION SPEAKS

Though never formally Pelagian, the Celtic Church's embrace
of creation and the divine spark within human nature allowed
for a prevailing sense that the gospel was strongly echoed in

[11] J.W.C. Wand, A History of the Early Church, p. 233.
[12] Anthony Duncan, The Elements of Celtic Christianity (Element, 1992),
p. 55.

creation. The created order spoke of the goodness of God. For those with eyes to see, the God of the Bible was to be found speaking through creation. This was the very way in which Patrick introduced the 'new God' to the daughters of the High King of Tara:

> When these questioned him as to who the New God was, and where he dwelt, Patrick replied, 'Our God is the God of all men, the God of Heaven and Earth, of sea and river, of sun and moon and stars, of the lofty mountain and the lowly valley, the God above Heaven, the God in Heaven, the God under Heaven; He has his dwelling round Heaven and Earth and sea and all that in them is. He inspires all, he quickens all, he dominates all, he sustains all. He lights the light of the sun; he furnishes the light of the light; he has put springs in the dry land and has set stars to minister to the greater lights ...' [13]

The notion that the divine might be associated with nature was no strange idea to pagan Celts. Gods and goddesses abounded in every tree, field, forest and stream. The thought of a High God who was placed above all other spiritual beings was also part of the pagan pantheon. The pre-Christian Celts also conceived of an otherworld that was mysteriously entwined with this world so that beings from the otherworld might come and inhabit the present world both to help and to menace humankind. These were clearly themes that a Christian

---

[13] Christopher Bamford, and William Marsh, *Celtic Christianity: Ecology and Holiness* (Floris Classics, 1986), pp. 18–19.

missionary could build upon and the Celtic Christian missionaries did so in several distinct ways.

First, nature represented a second book, alongside scripture
which could be read by those who knew how to look. This is
not the same as a mere natural religion because scripture, with
its divine revelation of the incarnation, represents the key by
which the second book of nature is opened and read. Philip
Sheldrake quotes Celtic literature to this effect: 'Seek no far-
ther concerning God; for those who wish to know the great
deep must first review the natural world ...' [14]

Second, the created order allows us to experience the presence of God around us. This sense of the immanence of God,
revealed in nature, is reflected in the great love that the Celts
had for the Psalms. Again, Sheldrake offers a quote from
Columbanus which typifies the approach of many Celtic
saints: 'Therefore God is everywhere, utterly vast, and everywhere nigh at hand, according to His own witness of Himself;
I am, He says, a God at hand and a God afar off.' [15]

Third, in seeking to make a connection between this 'new
God' that was being introduced and the natural world, the
Celtic saints looked for sympathetic and familiar themes in
the Bible as a whole and in the history of the people of Israel in
particular. For example, the theme of the land, so important
in Celtic culture, is consciously identified with the promised
land of Israel. The idea of fertility or the goodness of the land
is likened to that land which flows with milk and honey
promised to Israel. The concept of the mountain as a holy place
where God might be encountered is powerfully recognised as

---

[14] Sheldrake, *Living Between Worlds*, p. 76.
[15] Ibid.

present in both Old and New Testament accounts of significant encounters with God.

Other pre-Christian Celtic themes arising from nature,
such as the sacred nature of water and trees, were also given
explicit Christian content. The river of life and the waters of
baptism were interpreted in this light. In much the same way
the Celts seized on references in scripture to the tree of life and
so give a specifically Christian meaning to the importance
attached to trees by the pre-Christian Celts. Even the Celtic
interest in birds and animals were given Christian motifs.
For example, in Celtic Christian spirituality the dove was frequently identified with the Holy Spirit. Although it is com-
monplace for the Holy Spirit to be depicted as a dove in the
wider Christian tradition, in Celtic depiction, the Holy Spirit
could also be represented as a wild goose.

In all these ways nature 'spoke' of the God of the Bible. So
the connection between the holiness of the saints and the
wholeness with which they viewed both humankind and the
created order made perfect sense. It was almost as though their
relationship with nature confirmed their saintliness. Holiness
did not set them apart from the world, rather it placed them
within a reconciling relationship with nature which itself served
to illustrate the very gospel of peace of which they spoke.

The connection between holiness and wholeness suggests
an underlying mysticism which certainly does characterise the
Celtic saints. But this is not the mysticism which we might
associate with a kind of ancient pantheism. The Celtic saints
were not occupied with an admiration of nature itself. The
natural world pointed beyond itself to a more important reality: to a sense of the presence of angels who protected and evil
spirits who threatened. These forces of good and evil were seen
as an ever-present part of the natural order.

For this reason, prayers of protection, not just from the natural forces of wind and sea, terrifying as they can be in their own right, but more particularly from the forces of evil, become a common feature of Celtic worship. The world of the Spirit and the spirits bind man and nature together in a close natural relationship which gives a constant sense of the abiding nearness of God. That closeness of God can be perceived or encountered by anyone. It is not the special preserve of the saint or the scholar or the priest. It does not depend upon knowledge so much as the imagination. It represents what one writer refers to as 'the mountain behind the mountain',[16] the sense that beyond our measuring of all physical facts lies a deeper, more profound reality that emerges from creation but points us to the Creator. In this sense, creation does not just speak of God in a rational way, as a kind of proof of his existence. Rather, it directs its message to the spirit within us, touching a deep well of knowing which is normally activated by beauty, by art, by music and by the warmth of human compassion.

Once again, the connection between a Celtic view of reality and a more Eastern Christian view is obvious, contrasting with that of the missionaries from Rome. Such a vision of the place of the spirit and the imagination, finds echoes in the astonishingly rich liturgies of Eastern Orthodoxy. At its best, Orthodox worship conveys a sense of awe, mystery and wonder which leaves participants unsure whether they are in heaven, on earth or caught up in clouds of wonder somewhere in between. The same truths are spoken of in the Western

[16] Noel O'Donoghue, *The Mountain Behind the Mountain* (T. & T. Clark, 1993).

Roman church too, but somehow there comes a tendency to intellectualise, to rationalise, to order and to legislate for that which can only be truly entered through the imagination and the senses.

We are left, therefore, with something of a sense of the difference between the Roman and Celtic missions, rather than a definition of difference. These were not two distinct doctrines so much as differences of feeling and experience. For the Celts, the created order was a dominating reality working in human imagination through which God could be encountered. One is left with the impression that for the Roman missions, the natural order was present but not important, clearly there as a proof of the power of the Creator but not acting as an abiding and mystical reality. No doubt, for Romans, the God who created should properly be adored and worshipped simply on the evidence of his handiwork, but the sense of his pervading goodness operating in and through the creation seems much less present. It could hardly be denied as a concept but its reality seems emptied of any mystical encounter.

8

MISSION AS POWER ENCOUNTER

The relationship between religion and power is a complex matter. Nowhere is this more apparent than when one religion encounters another. The issues of power, protection and privilege arise when conversion is on the agenda. Spirituality and power are intimately connected and it is never the case that secular authorities stand on the sidelines as impartial observers. To pretend to be a neutral observer carries an implicit spiritual value system which may only become apparent when the supposed tolerance of such a stance itself comes under scrutiny. A position of supposed neutrality itself declares that no stance is necessary because religion has no power; it makes the implicit claim that religion does not matter enough for any particular stance to be needed. Detached impartiality is actually a declaration of power over religion.

Apart from its relationship with the secular authorities religion has an implicit power of its own, not just because religions imply a degree of institutional life, but more particularly because the very idea of the holy carries within it a notion of power. Rudolf Otto called the idea of the holy the *mysterium tremendum.*[1] The mystery, the awesomeness, the feeling of otherness that leads to a sense of a tremendous power that can never be entirely penetrated or tamed, this and more is contained in the notion of the holy. Religious ideas such as these lay claim on the minds, hearts and souls of humanity to a degree that secular rulers can feel themselves to be impotent in the face of such feeling.

In its early penetration of the British Isles, Christianity had no help from the secular powers, indeed it was strictly illegal. But, following Constantine's edict in 313, Christianity, at least in theory, enjoyed official patronage. This was far from being a decisive factor in the spread of the faith in Britain. Certainly it removed the fear of persecution and even death but it did not guarantee the status of Christianity with those who still adhered to pagan faiths.

Following the demise of the empire and the arrival of the new Saxon peoples, Christianity reverted to its earlier status of an endangered minority faith. In Ireland and parts of Scotland where Christianity had never had any state patronage its position in relation to the existing pagan beliefs was full of tension. The roots of that tension sprang from the role of the existing pagan faiths in the community and culture of Celtic society.

The pattern of pagan belief was very typical of many nature religions. The complex art of the druids bound together the key areas of the relationship between an essentially rural people and the world of nature. Their magical powers guaranteed the power of the various kings, especially in battle, and

---

[1] Rudolph Otto, *The Idea of the Holy* (OUP, 1923). As already mentioned, although this book was written such a long time ago it is still considered – albeit through the filter of political correctness – to be a seminal text, and is often quoted.

above all they secured the relationship between the living and the dead. None of these three concerns could be seen in isolation from each other: they were part of a single living system of belief. To call the ancient patterns of belief into question was to challenge a social and cultural system, not merely to debate theology.

It is clear that those most directly threatened by the arrival of Christianity were the priests or druids. Certainly, the role of the druids in opposing Patrick in Ireland and Columba in Scotland form part of the hagiography of each of these saints. The presentation of these stories indicates that the respective power of each adversary was a central issue. Following Columba's visit to convert King Brude of the Picts, Adamnan records an encounter with the druid Briochan who functioned as a close advisor to the king. After enquiring when Columba intended to set sail following his visit, Briochan threatened Columba with an unfavourable wind. Columba invoked the power of God. Adamnan continues:

> That same day, the saint, accompanied by a large number of followers, went to the long lake of the river Nesa (Loch Ness), as he had determined. Then the Druids began to exult, seeing that it had become very dark, and that the wind was very violent and contrary. Nor should we wonder, that God sometimes allows them, with the aid of evil spirits, to raise tempests and agitate the sea. For thus legions of demons once met in the midst of the sea the holy bishop Germanus, whilst on his voyage through the Gallican channel to Britain, whither he was going from zeal for the salvation of souls, and exposed him to great dangers, by raising a violent storm and causing great darkness whilst it was

yet day. But all these things were dissipated by the prayers of St. Germanus more rapidly than his words were uttered, and the darkness passed away.

Our Columba, therefore, seeing that the sea was violently agitated, and that the wind was most unfavourable for his voyage, called on Christ the Lord, and embarked in his small boat; and whilst the sailors hesitated, he the more confidently ordered them to raise the sails against the wind. No sooner was this order executed, while the whole crowd was looking on, than the vessel ran against the wind with extraordinary speed. And after a short time, the wind, which hitherto had been against them, veered round to help them on their voyage, to the intense astonishment of all. And thus throughout the remainder of that day the light breeze continued most favourable, and the skiff of blessed man was carried safely to the wished-for haven.

Let the reader therefore consider how great and eminent this venerable man must have been, upon whom God Almighty, for the purpose of manifesting His illustrious name before a heathen people, bestowed the gift of working such miracles as those we have recorded.[2]

The important part of Adamnan's account revolves around the words 'while the whole crowd looked on'. The demonstration of miraculous power to rival and better the miracle-working magic of the druids represents a critical evangelistic motif.

---

[2] Adamnan, *Life of Saint Columba* (Llanerch Enterprises, 1988), XXXV, pp. 94–5.

The same contest can be repeated in the lives of many other saints. One writer comments on the relationship of Patrick with the druids by noting: 'There is frequent mention of them [the druids] in the texts. Patrick waged an unceasing combat with them. "He warred against hard-hearted druids; he crushed the proud with the help of our Lord of fair heaven. He purified Ireland's meadow-lands," so we read in an ancient hymn.'[3]

The mention of the purification of the meadowlands is an important element, not just because of the particularly close relationship that the Celtic saints felt for nature, but especially because of the pagan Celtic custom of human sacrifice to bestow fertility on a given field.[4] There is a suggestion that part of the evangelisation undertaken by the Celts relates to the undoing of such acts through intercession for the purification of the land.

POWER ENCOUNTER IN THE PHYSICAL LANDSCAPE

Throughout the Celtic lands we can see two very different physical examples of the encounter between Christianity and earlier pagan beliefs. The first relates to connectivity or continuity, and the second to a more hostile engagement which emphasises a more radical discontinuity or power encounter.

We have already seen the extent to which many natural features were important in Celtic pagan worship. Streams, groves, woods and wells all feature in what was essentially a

---

[3] Louis Gougaud, *Christianity in Celtic Lands* (Sheed & Ward, 1932), p. 15.
[4] Ibid., p. 17.

nature religion. The pre-Christian Roman invaders, who in many respects had similarities in their basic approach to the gods, were not generally sympathetic to the natural element in Celtic worship. A number of accounts tell of how sacred woods were chopped down by the Romans – by Caesar near Marseilles, and by Suetonius Paulinus on Anglesey, to name two such examples.[5] Other places of worship, especially wayside shrines, were simply replaced by dedications to Roman gods.

The Celtic Christian missionaries seemed much more sensitive in their approach to many of these natural features. Wells in particular were not destroyed but were given Christian assignations, sometimes derived from the Celtic saint who first evangelised that particular area. This may have been because of the close association in Christianity of water with healing and with salvation. From the healing of Naaman to the pool of Siloam, water offers a powerful symbolism in relation to the healing work of God. The basic conviction of the Celts that God is good, that he has made a good world and that he intends well-being for those who dwell on the earth, allowed them to see worth in God's creation. At this point there is a degree of connectivity and continuity with the former religious beliefs and practices of the pagan Celts.

It is much more questionable whether that same continuity extended to that other obvious manifestation of pagan worship, the standing stones. It needs to be said that there is a debate on this matter. Some would take the view that the existence of many standing stones on which are carved both pre-Christian and Christian religious symbols demonstrates

---

[5] M. Dillon and N. Chadwick, *The Celtic Realms* (Weidenfeld & Nicolson, 1967), p. 138.

continuity and accommodation, a basically tolerant view in relation to earlier beliefs. One author argues for the continuity theme on the basis of 'the re-use of an old site, the familiarity of an old pair of slippers-syndrome'.[6] Such an argument suggests that it was relatively easy to move from one faith to another, from druid to saint (both holy), and from the conversion of a pagan worship site to a Christian place of worship.

But a contrary view is also possible. If it were the case that standing stones were not mere markers of territory as some maintain, but represented centres of worship and possibly places where human sacrifices were conducted, then accommodation would not have been easy, either from the perspective of the pagans or from that of the new missionaries. Viewed in such a way, these were not simply places to meet, so much as centres of pagan power. For the Celtic Christians immersed as they were in the Old Testament as well as the New, such stones were easily identified with the 'high places' so notorious in the life of the people of Israel and Judah.

We have no documentary evidence on the exact way in which these stones were regarded by the early Celtic missionaries. What we do have is extensive archaeological evidence which suggests that large numbers of the more significant standing stones or circles either had Christian symbols carved upon them or they were removed and used in the building of nearby churches. On other occasions, church buildings with their surrounding sacred ground were established on the same sites. Why should this be done? Was it an example of the incorporation of earlier beliefs or the overturning of them? Was it simply that as the Christian message spread these

---

[6] Marianna Lines, *Sacred Stones, Sacred Places* (Saint Andrew Press, 1992), p. xi.

ancient sites became abandoned and it was convenient to build churches on them? Or is it more likely that some kind of power encounter took place similar in feel to the meeting of Elijah with the prophets of Baal on Mount Carmel? Was the carving of crosses and Christian symbols on pagan worship centres indicative of a perceived and actual shift of power from earlier beliefs to a new faith? If so, this suggests a more radical discontinuity in the process of conversion, with power as a central issue.

There are some grounds for believing that the theme of discontinuity is more likely than a gradual easing from one faith to another. First, there is evidence, as in the accounts of Columba and Patrick of considerable and possibly violent hostility between the druids and the Christian missionaries and, by implication, with pagan belief systems. One account of the life of St Samson tells the dramatic story of an encounter between Samson and a predatory serpent that had held the people of a particular area in fear. It is clear that the serpent acted as a symbol of deeper occultic powers. The binding of the serpent within a small circle into which the cross is placed indicates the nature of the encounter. We learn that Samson carved the sign of the cross on a standing stone with his own hand.[7]

The hostility between these rival power centres is easily transferred to the unambiguous symbols of the respective cult. To incorporate the sacred worship site of another faith into your own newer worship site implies the assertion of power more than a kind of easy familiarity factor. By contrast, a well or a spring is potentially ambiguous in its meaning – we all

---

[7] For further information see Douglas Dales, *Light to the Isles* (Lutterworth Press, 1997), p. 47.

need to drink water, we all see the value of healing – and hence it is possible to see how such a symbol can be reinterpreted in the new tradition.

Second, the great hero of the Celtic missionaries, Martin of Tours, had inspired a tradition of antagonism towards pagan temples.[8] It is clear from the accounts of Martin's exploits in the destruction of temples that this violence was often resisted. Clearly, he saw the issue in terms of a spiritual contest rather more than a practical blow dealt to a rival religion. Martin had the advantage of working in a part of the empire and at a time when Christians still enjoyed protection from the Roman authorities. Although he might incur the wrath of the local population, at least the Christian faith enjoyed the patronage of the emperor. The situation of the early Celtic missionaries in the British Isles was often more precarious. There were few if any pagan temples as such, but the standing stones served the same function. The sites did not need to be destroyed physically but they did need to be overcome spiritually. The carving of Christian symbols onto stones that had been used in pagan worship represented the victory of the cross.

Third, the place of the miraculous is very important in the context of the encounters between Christians and pagans. The very event of a miracle implies a degree of discontinuity. God's action, dramatic change, the entry of the unexpected, these are all elements in an encounter that vindicates truth or righteousness. One example from the ministry of St Martin illustrates the place of the miraculous in much the same way that it is portrayed in many accounts of the Celtic saints.

---

[8] See Christopher Donaldson, *Martin of Tours: The Shaping of Celtic Spirituality* (Routledge, 1980), ch. 12.

The story relates to the destruction of a temple that had been built to give honour to a sacred pine tree. The temple in question was in a rural area near Marmoutier and the implication is that unlike the more Roman urban areas, the population had retained a more pagan Celtic religious system. The local population had little if any objection to Martin's destruction of the temple – buildings can be rebuilt and were not really imbedded in a Celtic religious belief structure. But when Martin wanted to cut down the tree itself, this was a different matter. The local leaders made a suggestion to Martin. They would cut down the tree if he would stand at the point where they thought the tree would fall. Clearly, if what he said about his God were true, then he would be protected and could come to no harm. Martin accepted the challenge and the contest began.

The story continues:

Accordingly since that pine tree was hanging over in one direction so that there was no doubt to what side it would fall on being cut, Martin, having been bound, is, in accordance with the decision of these pagans, placed in that spot where, as no one doubted, the tree was about to fall. They began therefore to cut down their own tree, with great glee and joyfulness, while there was at some distance a great multitude of wondering spectators.[9]

The story contains dramatic and familiar themes. Martin's followers were anxious, but he was confident and put his trust in

---

[9] Ibid., p. 110.

God. Most important of all, when the deliverance from danger took place, pagan and Christian alike believed a miracle had occurred. Then, numerous conversions took place, 'For there was hardly one of that immense multitude of heathens who did not express a desire for the imposition of hands, and abandoning his impious errors, made a profession of faith in the Lord Jesus.'[10]

The various accounts of the Celtic saints stress the place of the miraculous in their ministries. It was an authentication of their message as well as a sign of holiness. The connection between the miraculous power of the saints and the conversion of those who witnessed the miracle is made again and again. For example, the Welsh saint Carannog, who is said to have followed Patrick to Ireland, in common with other saints began to build a monastery. In doing so, he asked a local chief, described as a tyrant in the tale, if he could use a particularly fine tree. (Might it have been a sacred tree?) The chief is reported to have told him that he could have the tree if he could make it fall by prayer. The legend suggests that this is exactly what happened and it was cut into four pieces for use in the foundations. The result is that the miracle 'caused the tyrant to believe and be baptised along with his subjects'.[11] The subjects of the chief had already been converted and by implication would have been baptised without him but for the miracle. The very act of baptism itself, especially in the dramatic form of total immersion, emphasises conversion and hence discontinuity with all that has gone before.

---

[10] Ibid., p. 111.
[11] Elissa Henken, *Traditions of the Welsh Saints* (D. S. Brewer, 1987), p. 153.

SIGNS AND WONDERS, ROMANS AND CELTS

It could be argued that even though the various power encounters between the Celtic missionaries and their pagan adversaries represented a compelling element in the establishment of the new faith, similar acts can also be documented amongst the missionaries from Rome. As we saw in the account of Adamnan earlier in this chapter in relation to Columba, the Celtic apologists did not hesitate to ascribe the miraculous to those whom we might identify with a more continental and Roman tradition such as Germanus. The issue from the perspective of the Celts was not that their heroes worked miracles while Roman missionaries did not. The miracles that were witnessed bore testimony to the power of the gospel, not to the bearer of the message. Rather, the place of the miraculous, the reality of a spiritual power encounter was much more important to the missionary activity of the Celts than it was to the Roman mission.

The place of miracles in the Roman tradition was certainly recognised. Medieval Western Catholic piety includes the performing of miracles in a wide variety of situations. However, the emphasis does seem to be somewhat different. It is frequently the case that miracles are seen as increasing the faith of the devout rather than as an instrument of power encounter in mission, though even in this case there are some examples of the miraculous being used in such a way. But for the most part, the forms of power used by the Roman missionaries in converting the heathen seem to confirm faith rather than being used to produce faith.

Three themes emerge. The first is that of the relationship between the power of the church and the secular authorities.

While it is true that in the English context the role of kings was crucial for both the Celtic and Roman missions the precise nature of that relationship was rather different. In both cases the invitation of kings resulted in missions being established. In the case of the mission of Augustine an invitation was issued by the King of Kent, while the Northumbrian mission of Aidan came from a specific invitation from the King of Northumbria. But there the similarities diverge.

The picture that we have of the Roman missions is that of a much greater degree of integration between the missionaries and the nobility of the land. As Douglas Dales puts it, 'where the king led those who sought his favour would follow with their households, not always for the deepest of reasons. Moreover such royal patronage inevitably integrated the bishop and his monks into the aristocratic establishment of the Kentish court ...'[12] Such an arrangement contrasts sharply with the friendship between Aidan and Oswald, which led the king to accompany Aidan on preaching missions to the poor in the kingdom where the king would act as an interpreter for Aidan's preaching.

Wilfrid, the English bishop whose arguments so decisively routed the Celtic church at Whitby, serves as an example to illustrate the Roman political involvement. Dales comments, 'As bishop of the kingdom he had become a great lord, wielding influence and patronage alike well outside the confines of the territorial kingdom.'[13] However, it could be argued that Columba had exercised considerable political influence as something of a kingmaker in Scotland. Is this therefore an artificial distinction?

---

[12] Dales, *Light to the Isles*, p. 82.
[13] Ibid., p. 125.

Indeed, the contrasts are not always clear. Both Celts and Romans were committed to upholding the simple monastic life as centres of spiritual power in mission. Both Augustine and Columba were monks. But while it is one thing to see the monastery as a resource of prayer for mission, it is quite another to site the mission itself in the monastery. Perhaps the best way to describe the difference is to see the Celts as seeking to exercise influence from the 'desert' of the spiritual community located outside the secular settlement, as compared with the Roman vision of influence from within the centre of secular life.

There is a considerable contrast between the location of the episcopal see at Canterbury – the political capital of Kent, and later that of London and York – and the siting of Lindisfarne, not too far from the royal castle of Bamburgh, but symbolically separated by the waters of the North Sea. The desert place located outside society provides a perspective from which a given culture can be judged, approached, critiqued and ultimately changed. The Roman approach to mission, locating it at the centre of cultural life, might appear to be better placed to influence society, as salt savours the dish, but it is just as likely to be overwhelmed by the culture as it is to bring dynamic change.

The second theme is that of the contrast between the power of the community and the power of organisation. For the Celts, the leader of the mission was always the abbot in his role as leader of a community of people. Bishops had their place and, on occasion, abbots were also bishops, but without doubt the abbot held the position of pre-eminence in the Celtic mission. For the Romans the key figure was undoubtedly the bishop, seen as the ruler of a diocese defined in territorial terms. The dominant concern of leaders such as Theodore, Archbishop of Canterbury, was with such matters as canon law, doctrine, ecclesiastical appointments and organisational detail. In an important sense, the power of men such as Theodore derived from their administrative ability.

For the Celts, power derived from the degree to which a life of holiness and wisdom allowed the abbot to act as an effective leader of the community. The inspiration of others more than their appointment and direction was crucial. There are very few cases of Roman missionaries aspiring to the life of a hermit in the manner that the Celtic saints often sought.

The third theme relates to the part played by the papacy itself. Both at Whitby and in many other encounters, the Roman church appealed to the authority, and by implication, the power of Rome, in their various arguments. In so doing they were appealing not just to the pope but indirectly to the emerging centres of cultural, religious and political influence that were emerging on the continent. There was an important sense in which the Roman missions were encouraging a connection between the continent of Europe and England. The appeal to be a part of a new European order had a power of its own.

By contrast, the inspiration and horizon of the Celtic church remained powerfully Irish. That connection was not unimportant in the cultural sense. For at least two hundred years after the Celtic missions began, it is possible to think of Irish scholarship as highly influential and significant. The title of the book How the Irish Saved Civilization is by no means fanciful in its somewhat provocative phraseology.[14] But once

---

[14] Thomas Cahill, How the Irish Saved Civilization: The Untold Story of Ireland's Heroic Role from the Fall of Rome to the Rise of Medieval Europe (Doubleday, 1995).

scholarship became strongly re-established amongst the Roman missions, both in England and in other European lands, the cultural theme was no longer as decisive. Whitby represented a clear choice: to continue to look to Ireland for intellectual, cultural and spiritual inspiration, or to look to the continent of Europe, inheritors of secular Greek and Roman thought as well as the intellectual and spiritual riches of the church fathers. The pioneering work of Celtic missions was gradually giving way to the emergence of a European Christendom, a new, holy, Roman Empire was arising.

9

MISSION AT THE MARGINS

Beginning with the ministry of Jesus, there has always been a recognition that the marginalised have a place of importance in relation to the gospel message lived out and preached by the church. Clearly, there have been many times when the church has been unfaithful in demonstrating that commitment, but it has rarely denied its importance. The gospels record the concern of Jesus for children, for social outcasts such as tax collectors and sinners, for women, for the poor, the sick and the afflicted.

Both the Roman and Celtic missions record an involvement and concern for all the groups which stood at the margins of society. Indeed, some of the pioneers of both Roman and Celtic missions knew what it meant to be oppressed. Patrick had worked as a slave while Pope Gregory had deliberately bought English slaves in Rome in order to train them as missionaries to their own people. Both Celtic and Roman missions laid emphasis on acts of charity towards the poor. But, while it is one thing to be aware of a duty to the poor, it is another to see the poor as having a place of importance in terms of the gospel itself.

CONCERN FOR THE POOR

There is a good deal of evidence that the Celts saw what happened to the poor as a critical element in terms of the authentication of the gospel message. Why should this be and how was such a concern expressed?

The heart of the experiential inspiration of the Celtic saints was that of the desert. The desert taught the embrace of poverty as a route to spiritual insight. On occasion the desert fathers took their preoccupation with poverty to extremes. An author who retells one of the stories of the desert fathers says the following:

> A great personage came from abroad to Scete carrying with him a lot of gold and he asked the abbas if he could give it to the brothers. The abbas said: 'The brothers don't need it.' As the other insisted, he placed a basket full of gold at the door of the church and said: 'Anybody who needs it – take some.' Nobody did. So the abbas told the stranger to take it away to give to the poor.[1]

The Celts had been inspired by stories such as these. Their own embrace of poverty was not to indicate that poverty was an acceptable state, anymore than their practice of fasting indicated that others should go hungry. Their separation from the cares of the world did not lead them to view society with indifference. Their lifestyle had a spiritual purpose, namely, to equip them to wrestle with the forces of darkness. Spiritual

---

[1] Peter France, *Hermits* (St Martin's Press, 1997), p. 36.

discipline enabled them to discern and combat the demonic and thus enlighten the souls of those they came to minister to. Encounters with the demonic were taken very seriously and victory over these forces suggested the reality of a holy life. For example, a story involving Adamnan tells of how a demon came in human form to undermine his preaching and teaching by asking him questions that had an evil intent. The story ends as follows:

> ... Adamnan looked at him angrily and immediately made the sign of the cross in his direction. Thereupon the trouble-maker disappeared, leaving his stench in the assembly. Thus all the crowd knew that he was a demon in human guise who had come to deceive the multitudes. And through his expulsion by Adamnan God's name was magnified.[2]

The power and authority of the Celts flowed from the battles that had been fought and won in the isolation of their ascetic life. That same experience of extreme conditions, desolation, isolation, barren places, the abandonment of comfort, gave them the position of those who could comment on society from afar. Viewed from such a perspective, all of humanity is indeed equal, not as a utopian statement of ancient communism, but because, having experienced extreme vicissitude, the saints could see that all are equal in the condition of their sinfulness. Compassion for all as sinners, compassion for the poor as bearers of unequal burdens issued from the Celtic separation from society and formed a central part of the preaching

---

[2] Herbert (ed.), *Life of Adamnan* (Irish Texts Society, 1988), LIV, p. 49.

and teaching of the Celtic saints. We see that concern mani-
fested in a number of ways.

First, the stories of the saints suggest that they spent a good
deal of time ministering to the poor. Nowhere is this more pronounced than in the account of the ministry of St Cuthbert,
where Bede writes:

> Moreover, he was wont to resort most commonly unto
> those places and preach in those hamlets lying afar off
> in steep and craggy hills, which other men had dread to
> visit, and which from their poverty as well as uplandish
> rudeness teachers shunned to approach. And yet he did
> so gladly give himself to godly travail, and laboured so
> diligently in careful teaching of them, that he would
> go out of the monastery and ofttimes not come home
> again in an whole week, sometimes not in two or three,
> at times not even in a full month; but tarrying in the
> hilly parts, he would call the poor folk of the country to
> heavenly things with the word of preaching as well as
> work of virtuous example.[3]

This kind of concern for the poor was by no means limited to
Cuthbert. The *Life of Columba*, written by Adamnan, features
a number of stories which centre on Columba's compassion for
the poor. Typical of these is the saint's encounter with Nesan:

> This Nesan, though very poor, joyfully received on
> one occasion the saint as his guest. And after he had

---

[3] Bede, *A History of the English Church and People* (Penguin, 1988), III, 17
and 19.

entertained him as hospitably as his means would
afford for one night, the saint asked him the number of
his heifers. He answered, 'Five.' The saint then said,
'Bring them to me that I may bless them.' And when
they were brought the saint raised his holy hand and
blessed them, and said: 'From this day thy five little
heifers shall increase to the number of one hundred
and five cows.' And as this Nesan was a man of humble
condition, having a wife and children, the saint added
this further blessing, saying: 'Thy seed shall be blessed
in thy children and grandchildren.' And all this was
completely fulfilled without any failure, according to
the word of the saint.[4]

Second, it is suggested that the example of the saints influenced others in their conduct towards the poor. Ray Simpson
retells a well-known story concerning Aidan:

Gentle Aidan kept no worldly possessions for himself.
If wealthy people gave him money, then he gave it
to the poor or used it to buy freedom for those who
had been sold into slavery – many of whom became
Christian followers. King Oswald, who invited Aidan
to Northumbria, shared Aidan's heart for the poor. He
was about to begin a banquet at his castle in Bamburgh
when he was told that a crowd was outside begging for
food. Oswald sent out the food from the table, and
even had the large silver dish broken up to be shared
among the poor people. Aidan was so impressed that

---

[4] Adamnan, *Life of Columba* (Llanerch Enterprises, 1988), XX, p. 94.

he held up the king's right hand and asked God that it might never perish.[5]

Simpson goes on to claim that 'In Ultan's day, we are told that there wasn't one destitute child in all Northumbria.'[6]

Third, there is evidence that the poor were brought into the monasteries of the Celts to be cared for and taught the elements of the Christian life. We have already seen that Aidan used gifts of money to ransom slaves and bring them into the care of the monastery. Some of these not only became Christians but monks and priests. It is likely that those who had been oppressed as slaves might have had an easy affinity with the poor during the course of their own ministry.

Even apart from the actual welcome into the monastery for care and training, there seems to have been a natural affinity between the poor and the settlements of the Celtic monks. The very construction of the monasteries encouraged such an affinity. Even Lindisfarne, famed as it was as a centre of Celtic spirituality, consisted of wood and wattle huts. In a large monastic centre, the individual buildings were relatively simple and small. Worship for the whole community might well be in the open if no single building could accommodate them.

Such simplicity contrasted dramatically with the buildings that the Roman missions aspired to. Bede describes the founding of a Roman monastery at Monkwearmouth:

And when not more than a year had passed after the foundation of the monastery, Benedict crossed the

---

[5] Ray Simpson, *Exploring Celtic Spirituality* (Hodder & Stoughton, 1995), p. 146.
[6] Ibid., p. 147.

ocean to France, where he required, procured, and brought away masons to build him a church of stone, after the Roman fashion which he always loved. And in this work, out of the affection he had for the blessed Peter in whose honour he wrought it, he shewed such zeal that within the course of one year from the time the foundations were laid, the roof was put on, and men might see the solemnities of mass celebrated therein. Further, when the work was drawing nigh to completion, he sent messengers to France, which should bring over makers of glass (a sort of craftsman till that time unknown in Britain) to glaze the windows of the church, its side-chapels and clerestory ... Moreover, this devout buyer, because he could not find them at home, took care to fetch from oversea all manner of things, to wit sacred vessels and vestments that were suitable to the ministry of the altar and the church.[7]

The affinity which the Celtic missionaries felt for the poor undoubtedly had the effect of rooting the gospel deeply within the life of the people. There remains a contrast between the mission of the Roman missionary Paulinus in Northumbria and that of the later Celtic mission begun by Aidan. Paulinus was invited by King Edwin of Northumbria, and Bede reports that large numbers of Edwin's subjects were baptised following the king's own conversion. But, following the defeat of Edwin by the pagan King Penda, Paulinus fled and it seemed that the

[7] Bede, 'Lives of the Abbots of Wearmouth and Jarrow', 5 in D. Farmer, *The Age of Bede* (Penguin, 1965), p. 189.

advances made for the gospel were largely reversed. A similar pattern of events took place in southern England following the death of Ethelbert.

Although it is certainly true that the Celtic missions did not face the replacement of a Christian king by the enthronement of a pagan successor in the same way that some of the Roman missions did, the extent to which the faith was established amongst the ordinary people, often in remote places, suggested that such a complete reversal in the fortunes of the Celtic church was much less likely. Indeed, the work of Celtic missions elsewhere suggests that the Celtic church was not dependent on royal patronage in quite the same way that the Roman missions had been. Ministry to the poor had a profound and practical effect in causing the gospel to be integrated in the life of the nation at a deep level.

THE PLACE OF WOMEN

Some writers have wanted to make significant claims for the place of women in the Celtic church. However, the issues are extremely complex and it is not wise to make too many general statements on the basis of a relatively small number of concrete examples. The primary difficulty is that we are dealing with two very different locations for the operation of the Celtic church. What happened when the Celtic missions were working in Celtic societies cannot be easily extended to their operation in Saxon societies. The role of women clearly differed between Celtic and Anglo-Saxon societies and we cannot assume that what happened in Ireland was identical to that which took place either in other Celtic lands, such as Wales and Scotland, and still less so within the missions to Anglo-Saxon lands.

Even within Celtic society, it would be wrong to assume that men and women were entirely equal in the twentieth-century Western understanding of equality between the sexes. Nor should we confuse equality before the law with similarity of roles. Irish law gave rights to both women and wives that do not seem to be echoed in the various Anglo-Saxon kingdoms. Irish society also gave inheritance rights to women which are certainly not to be found within Anglo-Saxon culture. We can therefore say that the roles of women are not significantly different between Celtic and Saxon societies, but that the status, and hence security, of women to act and be heard was significantly greater within Celtic custom. However, even here we must be careful not to claim too much. St Patrick observed that 'Irish virgins had to endure the reproaches and persecution of their kinsfolk, some being threatened with slavery, others subjected to constant molestation.'[8] Security for women was within the context of marriage and family and not purely in their own right as women.

Having declared such a caveat there were significant differences between the treatment of women in Anglo-Saxon society as compared with Celtic society and these may well account to a significant degree for the apparently more pronounced part that women played within the broad stream of the Celtic missions. Two women in particular – one Irish, the other an Anglo-Saxon operating broadly within the Celtic tradition – illustrate the nature of this contribution. Their stories are worthy of some consideration.

---

[8] Louis Gougaud, *Christianity in Celtic Lands* (Sheed & Ward, 1923), p. 87.

St Brigid

As with so many of the Celtic saints the various hagiographies
leave us with what one historian has called an 'incoherent'
account of her life.[9] There were other famous Brigids, for
example in Wales, and the various stories of these saints easily
become confused. Another historian believes that the Welsh
St Brigid was herself a conglomeration of three Brigids, namely
another St Brigid of North Wales, and a St Brigid of Kildare,
not to mention a selection of pre-Christian Celtic goddesses.[10]

Despite these difficulties, there are some elements in her
story about which we can be reasonably certain and which
mark her out as a significant figure within the Celtic church.
The various accounts of her birth suggest that her mother was
a slave by the name of Broicsech, within the household of
King Dubtach, the King of Leinster. Having become pregnant
by Dubtach, Broicsech endured jealousy from Dubtach's wife
until it was no longer possible for her to remain in the household. There is a claim that Brigid was actually brought up by a
druid who had the wisdom to recognise that she was destined
for greater things than her mother had known. There is also a
claim that she was baptised by St Patrick and in due course
returned to live in her father's royal household. She was reput-
edly born in the year 455 and although we cannot be certain
of this date, she certainly conducted her ministry during the
latter half of the fifth century.

It seems that Dubtach had some cause to regret Brigid's
arrival in his household. She revealed a tendency to give her

---

[9] Ibid., p. 85.
[10] Patrick Thomas, *Candle in the Darkness* (Gomer Press, 1993), pp. 107–10.

father's property to the poor and needy. One particular incident caused her father to be more angry than usual. Apparently Brigid gave her father's sword to a leper who came to ask for help. This action almost caused her father to sell her into slavery![11]

After Brigid refused to be married off to a local nobleman she went instead to become a nun. One can imagine some relief on the part of her father! Although we do not know the precise detail of her progress as a nun, we can say that she came to found a monastery at Kildare and it was from this institution that her fame spread. The story surrounding her founding of the monastery suggests something of the determination for which she was noted. According to legend the local chief at Kildare initially refused to give her land on which to build her monastery. When she would not stop asking, he eventually agreed to give her a piece of land no bigger than the size of his cloak. When laid on the ground, the cloak grew until it filled an area that was more than sufficient for the monastery she had in mind.

We are told that Kildare had a special significance for the pagans of the area because of the presence of a group of oak trees that had cultic importance. This may account for the initial reluctance of the local chief to give her the land she required. In any case, the fact that she built on such a site seems to have added to her reputation.

The house that was established at Kildare became a double monastery, one house for men and another for women. Needless to say, Brigid ruled over both, enlisting the help of a bishop, Conlaed, who assisted her with the male house. The

---

[11] Edward Sellner, *Wisdom of the Celtic Saints* (Ave Maria Press, 1993), p. 71.

legends that surround her suggest that in addition to her unusual role in supervising a double monastery, she was also ordained as a bishop.

The account of this event is unclear as to its precise meaning. One suggestion is that the bishop who ordained her did so because of the appearance of a pillar of fire from her head to the roof of the church. Others have suggested that the bishop simply made a mistake and possibly because of poor eyesight or a forgetful mind, inadvertently read the wrong part of the service, so mistakenly ordaining her as a bishop. We cannot know what really happened and not too much should be made of the event as there is no real evidence that she operated in such an office. But what we can say is that her reputation and influence was significant for the emerging Irish church, so much so, that she is often referred to as 'the Mary of the Gael'.

St Hilda

Hilda, the daughter of the Northumbrian nobleman Hereric, nephew of King Edwin, seemed also to have been a formidable personality. Thanks to the writing of Bede we know a good deal more about Hilda than we do of Brigid. She was born in 614 and converted through the ministry of Paulinus in 627. At the age of thirty-three she decided to become a nun, possibly inspired in part by her sister Hereswith, who was then living in a monastery. Her initial intention had been to spend some time in East Anglia and then to travel to one of the monasteries in Gaul.

While she was still in East Anglia, she came under the influence of Aidan and was persuaded to move to a location on the northern side of the Wear. From there she moved to Hartlepool, and soon became the abbess. Following a time at

Hartlepool she established another monastery at Tadcaster. From there she eventually moved to establish the famous house at Whitby where she remained until her death in 680.

As with Brigid, Hilda ruled over monasteries which contained both men and women. And what outstanding men were formed by her tuition. At least five became bishops, including the famous John of Beverley, and Wilfrid, the later champion of the Roman rule. The poet Caedmon was also instructed by Hilda at Whitby. Bede records that both ordinary people and kings came to consult Hilda 'in their difficulties', so great was her reputation.

Although we could certainly argue that these two women were unusual exceptions, it seems that there were others who also ruled over similar monasteries. The historian Gougaud notes that St Salaberga, Itta, Gertrude and Burgundofara also headed similar double monasteries and that these women were also operating under the influence of Irish missionaries.[12] In short, these institutions were sufficiently numerous for us to suggest that women did play a very important part in the overall mission of the Celts.

Taken together with the very easy relationship that the Celtic saints enjoyed with the poor and with slaves, and bearing in mind the extent to which the nobility did not seem to enjoy a place of special privilege within the Celtic mission, it is not too fanciful to suggest that there was something in the spirituality of the Celts that saw all of humanity as brothers and sisters in the cause of Christ. In this, the Celts seem to share a good deal in common with the desert fathers, whose spirituality acted as an inspiration for their ministry. The

---

[12] Gougaud, *Christianity in Celtic Lands*, p. 86.

desert fathers seemed to go to extraordinary lengths to avoid being courted by the rich and famous. One story amongst many others taken from the desert fathers makes this point:

> Another time, another nobleman came to see him [the abbas Simon]. The servants came before and said to the abbas: 'Abbas, get ready, the nobleman, who has heard of you, comes for your blessing.' And he said: 'Yes, I'll get ready.' He put on his patched garment and, taking bread and cheese in his hands, sat at the entrance enthusiastically eating. When the nobleman arrived with his train, he scorned him, saying; 'Is this the anchorite we've heard of?' And they turned and went back home.[13]

Something of this same apparently perverse behaviour seems to mark out the Celtic saints as those who so valued humility and simplicity that those on the margins of society were equal beneficiaries of the gospel message the saints lived and preached.

---

[13] Peter France, *Hermits*, p. 28.

10

TRAVELLERS FOR CHRIST

The Celtic saints – unlike the desert fathers whom they admired, or St Martin who acted as inspiration for many – travelled to an astonishing extent. In this respect they stood in complete contrast to the very figures to whom they looked for guidance. The desert fathers did not travel and St Martin remained largely close to his single base at Tours. To some degree, the fame of both St Martin and the desert fathers rested on their withdrawal to a single place.

While some have suggested that the Celts were travellers because they were looking for their own desert in an overseas context, this explanation does not take account of the fact that many kept travelling. They had temporary resting places, some on islands, a few on mountains, others in isolated country areas, but these were not necessarily permanent homes. Some have called them wanderers and it is certainly true that they were prepared to be led in a remarkable and unpredictable fashion. But their travelling was not aimless – it had a clear purpose. They were truly pilgrims, or *peregrini*, but of a particular kind.[1]

---

[1] For the best overview of the travels of the Celtic saints see Roisin Mheara, *In search of Irish Saints: The Peregrinatio pro Christo* (Four Courts Press, 1994).

Columbanus represents an archetypal figure for the Celtic pilgrim. His biographical details have already been sketched in Chapter 3 but we should add some other elements to this initial picture. Columbanus is an important figure in Celtic studies for at least three reasons. First, he was a relatively early figure in the Celtic exodus. Although younger than Columba he was roughly his contemporary but, unlike Columba and many earlier Celtic saints, he travelled to entirely foreign fields. Second, as we have already noted, the power of his personality, combined with his force as a scholar and possibly his organising ability, caused a large number of monasteries either to be founded by him or to operate under his broader aegis. Third, almost uniquely amongst the early saints, there still exists a significant body of his authentic writings. Among these are sermons, poetry, letters and sermons. To this original material we can add a biography written by Jonas, who came to Bobbio just three years after his death. We know that Jonas travelled to the places where Columbanus worked, and spoke personally to those who had known him as part of his preparation for the biography, written around the year 630.

The picture we have of Columbanus is of someone who is fiercely independent. Of course, that element may have been inherent in his personality and one can debate whether it is those of independent temperament who are likely to go on missionary journeys, or whether the journey itself births the tendency towards passion. Most likely the two interact. But it is also true that pilgrimage of the type embraced by Columbanus, and others like him, inherently contains an extreme element. This was not an excursion, a grand tour of the continent; it was a much more serious matter – this was a journey for Christ.

It was this element of extravagant passion that was also so contagious for many. One writer suggests that 'the penalty of holiness was popularity'.[2] That might sound strange to the modern ear, where stories of rags to riches seem to matter more than stories in which the hero gives up wealth to serve others. Many modern heroes are celebrated for their notoriety rather than their goodness. Yet there was a strange attraction in that Columban community, 'living together in ideal brotherliness and in strictest discipline'.[3] Such community experiences breed the expectancy that God can do anything that he chooses. Passionate commitment produces the willingness to take immense risks. Some of those risks were demonstrated in prayers for the sick. The dramatic healing of the sick instantly changed the saints' status with the surrounding populations.

The boldness of the pilgrim bound to fellow travellers in community does not end with the boundary of the monastery walls. Columbanus was famed for other extravagant actions, some of which produced conflict both religious and secular. In addition to writing to Pope Gregory to instruct him on the proper date of Easter (around the year 600), an admonition that failed to produce any noticeable change, the fierce independence of the pilgrim for Christ brought him into considerable conflict with various bishops.

The mission in Burgundy at Annengray, was approximately ten years old and experiencing considerable success when the local bishops felt that it was time to rein him in. Columbanus was summoned to appear before a synod of bishops at Chalons sur Saone in 603 to answer a variety of charges. He did not appear but sent a letter instead. The correspondence makes it clear that he did not feel obliged to come under their authority

[2] See John McNeill, *The Celtic Churches: A History* AD 200 to 1200 (University of Chicago Press, 1974), p. 159.
[3] Ibid., p. 159.

at all. This was no doubt because in part he had in mind the custom of his own land in seeing bishops as less important than abbots. But his call as a pilgrim for Christ is also mentioned and the implication is that this call, the reason for his presence amongst them, takes precedence over any authority that the bishops might have over the settled Christian community.

That same boldness caused him to speak to the local rulers in a less than diplomatic manner. The king of Burgundy, Theuderic II, had two illegitimate sons. Brunhilda, his grandmother, and the real power behind the throne, asked Columbanus to bless Theuderic's illegitimate sons. Possibly she was used to the clergy obeying her command, but she had had not taken account of the independent spirit of Columbanus. One writer sums up the resultant confrontation in these few well-chosen words: 'He came before the court in high anger, cursed the boys as the offspring of harlotry, and foretold their fate never to come to royal power. Theuderic had him seized and taken to Besançon, where he found opportunity to preach to a numerous band of condemned prisoners.'[4]

The same cantankerous spirit was evident when Columbanus came eventually to northern Italy, to Bobbio in Lombardy. Here he was confronted by the presence of the new rulers of that part of Italy, the Lombards. They had earlier adopted an Arian form of Christianity, an anathema to Columbanus.[5] He spoke against the beliefs of the Lombards, a dangerous occupation since Arianism had also been adopted by the then King of Lombardy, Agilulf. Not content with preaching from the relative safety of his monastery, he preached also at court,

---

[4] Ibid., p. 161.
[5] For a good exploration of Arius and his supposed heresy see Rowan Williams, *Arius* (DLT, 1987).

eventually convincing the Queen. By now Columbanus was in his seventies and eventually died peacefully, a hero and an independent spirit to the end.

Columbanus was not the sole Celtic figure travelling across Europe. A former companion of Columbanus, St Gall, laboured near Lake Zurich amongst the Alemanni. St Fursa worked first in East Anglia and then moved on to found a monastery at Lagny near Paris and then at Peronne. St Kilian came to Würzburg around the year 643, and St Ursus preceded Columbanus by travelling from Ireland to the area of Digne in southern France before moving to Aosta across the Alps where he too worked amongst the Arian Lombards. Another colleague from Ireland working in the same region was St Fridian who established a monastery at Lucca. The names we know are almost certainly vastly outnumbered by the work of those whose names we can never know, all part of the restless, independent travellers for Christ, most of whom came from Ireland itself.

THE THREE MARTYRDOMS

The Celts spoke of three martyrdoms. The red martyrdom is fairly self-explanatory. As the colour suggests, red stands for sacrifice or death. Red martyrdom represents therefore the traditional Christian understanding of a believer's death for the sake of Christ. It has often been remarked that the Celts rarely experienced red martyrdom. As compared with some of the more violent persecutions of the early Christian era, or even with some situations in modern times, death for the faith was rare amongst the Celtic saints.

But such a reality has to be seen in context. A number of writers have noted the absence of martyrdoms in such a way as almost to suggest that somehow the Celts had it easy. The reality is more complex. First, it is true to say that few amongst the missions from Rome met with grisly deaths either. Persecution of the kind that produces martyrs was not really a factor in the sixth, seventh and eighth centuries. The Christian faith was well regarded even by those who had not adopted it. The paganism practised by the new Germanic tribes entering Europe was of that type which liked to keep its options open. It neither killed the priests of other faiths nor were the old priests or believers put to death when leaders became Christians, at least during these centuries. There seemed to be no shortage of courage and even confrontation in the mission of the Celts. The absence of red martyrs might be better seen as a sign of their success in impressing those they went to win rather than an implied failure of conviction and hence lack of death.

Moreover, there was to come a time and circumstance when the red martyrdom was all too common amongst Celtic believers and leaders in the church. In the ninth century the frequent invasions of the Vikings in Scotland, northern England, Ireland and Wales, had a devastating impact on the church. Whole communities of monks and nuns were killed. It is even said that the wife of Thorgeis, the sea king, incanted spells at the high altar in Armagh.[6] Changed conditions rather than a difference in commitment brought many to experience red martyrdom.

The Celts spoke also of a green and a white martyrdom. There is some debate as to whether there really is a great difference between these latter two martyrdoms. In both cases there is a connection with separation from that which is loved in the

---

[6] Ian Finlay, *Columba* (Chambers, 1992), p. 229.

context of penance. White martyrdom involves separation from everything and everyone that is loved. That inevitably means separation from one's clan and country. Although it is possible to see how one can travel to another part of the same country there is still a strong suggestion that white martyrdom can be better accomplished by travelling overseas, never to return. However, white martyrdom is in a sense a voluntary matter, something willingly embraced out of love for Christ.

Green martyrdom contains all that has been outlined in white martyrdom but it also includes an element of separation from inner desires. It seems to have been used in more serious cases of sin and may have been an imposed penance. We cannot know how many of those who travelled across the continent of Europe did so in relation to the white martyrdom or the green martyrdom. What we do know is that few expected to return. The state of pilgrimage was a permanent fact, an exile, not merely a journey from which one returned after a time. In this context it is easy to see why Columba was so reluctant to return to Ireland to settle a dispute. The sods of earth he cut to place upon his feet were not just the actions of a truculent and awkward man, they also enabled him to preserve something of the integrity of his commitment to permanent exile. The story that he could not settle until he could be sure that nothing could be seen of Ireland even from the highest hill in Iona, does not indicate a man who had a vindictive or regretful view of his homeland; it only speaks of the commitment to a white or green martyrdom – to complete separation.

In this respect, the Celtic approach to *peregrinatio* was very different from the earlier or later understandings of pilgrimage.[7] Pilgrimage had started as a kind of religious curiosity, an interest to see the Holy Land, once that became possible. The early focus had always been on the places spoken of in the Bible, and in Jerusalem in particular. It was only later that pilgrimage to other sites, such as Rome, began to grow in popularity. Although some of the Celts travelled to Rome, and indeed as far as the Holy Land, such journeys were for a variety of reasons and not *pro Christo* (for Christ) in the way that the lifelong *peregrinatio* was.

As already mentioned, the desert fathers, so dear to the hearts of the Celts, saw their exile as a kind of journey. It was a journey within, to do battle with strange spiritual forces both within and without their own being. In some ways this desert exile was closer to the *peregrinatio* of the Celts, but the restless wandering of the Celts, the sense that no place on earth could ever be a permanent home, marked their pilgrimage out as different from the desert saints.

No matter how dangerous the medieval pilgrimage might be, and it frequently was, pilgrims always hoped to return even if they set their affairs in order lest death met them on the way. The Celts set out with no thought of return. Their hearts were set on the improvement of their own life, just as modern pilgrims hope for some measure of self-discovery or spiritual enrichment in their journeys to places of spiritual significance. But spiritual growth was still not their primary goal.

---

[7] A range of pilgrimage narratives through the history of Christianity can be found in Martin Robinson, *Sacred Places, Pilgrim Paths: An Anthology of Pilgrimage* (HarperCollins, 1997).

THE INSPIRATION FOR
PEREGRINATIO

The question as to why so many Celts embarked on a white martyrdom is important for understanding the nature of the Celtic church. Of course, the biblical images that suggest the significance of pilgrimage were well known to the Celts as they are to all Christians. The picture of Abraham setting out from his home in obedience to the call of God was a familiar text. The image of the people of Israel wandering in the desert with only a pillar of fire by night and a cloud by day to guide them is powerfully suggestive. Perhaps even more poignant is the call of Christ to all those who would follow him to take up their cross and be ready for a lifelong pilgrimage of suffering, even to the point of being ready for martyrdom. Such an image was powerfully compelling for the radical Celtic disciple.

The image of journey is repeated in the New Testament even apart from the gospels: the example of St Paul and his missionary journeys, the call of the author of the Hebrews to travel in faith, and the exhortation of Paul to run the race to the point of completion. All these passages suggest that the true Christian life is a life of pilgrimage. But not all believers have embraced *peregrinatio* in the way that the Celts did. Why then was the idea of the *peregrinatio* so compelling to these generations of missionaries?

Some have pointed to the apparently natural tendency of Celtic peoples to be wanderers, a tendency that is seen even today in the widespread dispersal of Celtic populations around the world. The presence of the sea around the Celtic homelands has caused a strong seafaring tradition to develop. The Celts were explorers and warriors. Their populations sought new lands to conquer and develop. But this same tendency can also be traced in other peoples. The sea-based journeys of the Vikings had some similar features but did not produce the same compulsion towards *peregrinatio*. What then was so particular about the Celtic understanding of the faith that led them to respond in such a way?

The key to understanding the urge towards *peregrinatio* lies in the unique fusion of a number of ideas within the Celtic conception of the faith. Four themes are important. First, as we have already mentioned, there is a connection with penitence. White or green martyrdom were forms of penance. The emphasis of the Celtic approach to the faith was to mix action with faith. So, although the Celts would recognise that sins had been forgiven by the action of Christ on the cross, they also saw that in living the Christian life this action demanded a response. The call to be baptised or even to confess sin was a positive human action designed to respond to the action of Christ in such a way that one's life changed. Penance was not seen as punishment so much as a positive action to bring change.

The Penitential of Cummean (c. 650) gives a list of twelve actions, beginning with baptism and ending with martyrdom, that are helpful in dealing with personal sin. The list seems to have been based on an older tradition, possibly going back as far as the early church father Origen,[8] and although Origen and the other fathers saw martyrdom as meaning literal death, the Celts reinterpreted this as also meaning *peregrinatio*. In the same way St Finnian of Clonard and, following him, Columbanus, reflected in their penitential exercises the need to deal with sin by positive replacement. So, instead of merely

---

[8] D. Mould, *The Celtic Saints* (Clonmore & Reynolds, 1956), p. 115.

attempting to root out a sin, they recommended replacing a sin with an opposite positive virtue. For example, the one who envies others needs to cultivate a spirit of charity, while those who are greedy should seek a gift of giving to others. This practical approach to faith saw permanent pilgrimage as a way of penance, not just to deal with past sins, but as a means of building a totally different way of living.

Second, for the Celt, the barrier between this life and the next was almost translucent. That was so in their pagan past. The high king was thought to be able to converse with those from the otherworld and their folklore was full of such stories. Celts would lend money to each other on the understanding that it would be repaid in the next life, a practice that bemused the Romans and would certainly be beyond the possibilities entertained by most bank managers. But the fact that they felt the barrier to be thin gave them a strong sense of the ever-present reality of heaven, a feeling that through their *peregrinatio* – their action in this life – the kingdom of God was constantly breaking through. Their boldness in embracing such a life, in speaking forcibly to kings and other rulers, of having scant regard for the authority of local bishops, was a reflection of their vision of heaven, more than a sign of being difficult individuals.

Third, for the Celtic Christians, a radicality of obedience was of great importance. It is hard to know precisely why this was the case. It may have been partly in the temperament of the people and perhaps those who look at some of the penitential aspects of modern Irish pilgrimage feel that it still is. It may also be related to a deep gratitude towards Christ for the awareness that the revelation of the great High King of Heaven represented such freedom from past fears that any journey, any cost, any sacrifice would be a small payment indeed. What we know is that the Celtic penitentials and monastic rules were far more severe than those in the various Benedictine foundations. Their chastisements seem harsh to a modern eye, their austerity challenging, to say the least. Their devotional practices are hard for us to understand, but in all of these matters there was a kind of radical commitment which the *peregrinatio* exemplified. To leave one's home, never to return, spoke of utter abandonment of self to a cause.

Fourth, the phrase 'for Christ' (*pro Christo*) is vital in understanding the *peregrinatio*. It was 'for Christ' that the pilgrimage was undertaken and not for self. This may seem a subtle point but it is an important one. The linkage with penance, understood wrongly, can easily be taken to mean that the *peregrinatio* was designed to deal with a self-centred obsession with personal sin. Had that been the case, then the journey itself would not have been necessary. Withdrawal into closed community would have been enough. But that was not the nature of the Celtic monastic life. These were journeys undertaken to live the Christian life, to exemplify it, to help others and to preach the good news about Christ. The resultant communities were ones which engaged with the world.

The desire to travel for Christ helped to keep the practice of *peregrinatio* positive in its outlook. Even though the idea of penance was designed to produce healthy spiritual lives without the *pro Christo* theme, a concern for penance alone might have produced a different kind of journey. Some writers have suggested that the journeys of the Celtic saints were not about mission but were in the first instance about penance.[9] Of course it is true that penance was a key element, but the

---

[9] For example, Finlay, *Columba*, p. 46.

motive to travel for Christ transforms the theme of penance in such a way that mission comes to the fore. The task of proclamation becomes the positive replacement for a life previously lived without devotion to Christ.

These four themes clearly resonate with each other and interrelate in such a way that the *peregrinatio* continued to inspire thousands of followers of Christ for more than two centuries. The wonder of that exodus is well expressed by John McNeill: 'That one small island should have contributed so rich a legacy to a populous continent remains one of the most arresting facts of European history.'[10]

But an exploration of the themes still does not explain exactly why there was such a vast and rich stream of *peregrini* at this time. To some extent it is always difficult to understand what drove particular movements in history. The reasons are inevitably imbedded within a given culture's self-consciousness in ways that are not easily unpacked. But a clue might well lie in the very extreme nature of the penitential exercises themselves. Our ever-present modern awareness of Freud might tempt us to conclude that guilt of the most morbid kind drove them. However, an overall look at the attractive quality of these individuals will not allow that kind of conclusion. Many of the Celtic saints were high-born individuals. A good number of the men, and possibly some of the women, might have been expected to be warriors at one time. As soldiers and leaders of others they would have been expected to undergo hardship of a kind scarcely imaginable to those of us living in the Western world of the twentieth century. Having become soldiers of Christ, might it not be the case that they would

---

[10] McNeill, *The Celtic Churches*, p. 175.

have welcomed and indeed required challenges of the most extraordinary kind?

Might it also be that they knew what it would take to conquer their own passions in the cause of Christ. Their involvement in a relatively recent past of pagan worship – an involvement that did not suddenly and altogether disappear with the Christianisation of Celtic lands – gave them a sharp awareness of the spiritual battles that they faced. It is no coincidence that many of the saints felt that they were engaging in battle with dark spiritual forces, demons and worse, during their times of prayer and penitence. The extreme asceticism they embraced was designed to equip them for spiritual battle in the way that physical endurance prepares the soldier for physical battles. The more severe the training the more elite the unit. The *pereginatio* may well have flowed from a profound awareness of these kinds of issues. The journey away from the claims of kith and kin might well have been part of the necessary external separation to allow an individual to produce the internal separation from profoundly harmful habits that was necessary to see the cause of Christ established. The urge to journey continued until the Norse invasions of Celtic lands brought mission to the homelands in a thoroughly unexpected way.

11

THE SIGNIFICANCE OF THE CELTS

 Most of the chapters of this book have attempted to give some information on the Celtic church. It would have been possible to say more, and especially to tell more of the individual stories of the saints, but it is also important to ask what the significance of their total story might be. From a purely historical point of view, the increase of information on the Celts has added to a broader revision of the general understanding as to how Christianity developed in Western lands.

Recent events in the history of Europe have forced us to reconsider what we mean by the term 'Europe'. In the period between the end of the Second World War and the fall of the Berlin Wall 'Europe' often meant the two very different Europes of West and East. The growing reunification of Europe allows us to look again at what a common European culture, history, heritage and home might mean. Europe can once more be seen as a culture which has interacted in particular ways with other cultures and continents in the world. The shift in focus from two Europes – one broadly liberal and democratic, the other communist and totalitarian – to a single Europe which sees itself as part of a broader Western culture, but distinct in particular ways from North America, allows a re-consideration of the elements that caused a common European story to emerge from the multiplicity of stories owned by the various tribes of Europe.

In this context, the contribution of the Celts is now better understood. They are no longer seen as simply forms of the faith that existed in Celtic lands, but which were then over-taken. Their active role in shaping large parts of Europe is now recognised. In a purely historical sense their role and reputation are rightly restored. But the present interest in the Celts seeks to go beyond a merely historical restitution. Their contribution is often vested with ideological significance. Learning from the Celtic contribution to the shaping of our past is just as challenging as restoring their place in history. There are at least three major understandings of that signifi-cance which need to be examined before attempting to learn some further lessons.

HIJACKING THE CELTS

There is always a need to exercise caution in interpreting his-tory. It is all too easy to read into history our own desires and hopes. It is very clear that there is both a Reformation and a Catholic view of Celtic history. A number of writers have noted the extent to which Reformation sources suggested that there had existed an original and pure Celtic church which had preceded the later Catholic influence. It does not take much imagination to see that the Reformers wished to be iden-tified with this supposedly original and pure church, the more so if the Reformer lived in those parts of the British Isles which still feels itself to be Celtic in culture and race. Donald Meek makes the following observation on such a trend: 'In fact, there are those in the Free Church of Scotland, no less, who look to that Celtic church of monks, anchorites and ascetics – that church of island fastnesses, hermitages, wheel-headed crosses, crucifixes and round towers – as its own lineal ancestor.'[1] He goes on to point out that such a rewriting of history is just that, a kind of historical revisionism.

In the same manner it is noticeable that in Ireland Catholic writers present Patrick not as the representative of a separate Celtic tradition, but as a figure fully sympathetic with continental Catholicism. In that sense Patrick was both a good Irishman (at least by adoption) and a good Catholic. Both pictures are of course true. The Celtic church was different in some respects from the church in Rome, but no more so than regional churches elsewhere in Europe at that time. Patrick was indeed a missionary who promoted a strongly Catholic faith but he did not feel himself to be under the authority of Rome in quite the way that current Irish prelates do. The fact is we cannot project our own causes onto the pages of history without distorting to some degree the story that we study. Patrick and the other Celtic saints neither anticipated a Reformation Protestantism nor a Counter-Reformation Catholicism. The categories of later historical experience are simply not appropriate for an earlier period so remote from the later battles of a divided Christendom. Patrick was neither a good Roman Catholic nor a good Presbyterian, neither a Nationalist nor an Orangeman.

---

[1] Donald Meek, 'Modern Celtic Christianity', *Scottish Bulletin of Evangelical Theology*, vol. 10, no. 1 (spring 1992), pp. 8–9.

ROMANTICISING THE CELTS

Just as Catholic and Protestant readings of the Celts might attempt to press them into ideological service, so too a romantic view of the Celtic past can distort what we see. The romanticism of the nineteenth century has further clouded the picture. The creation of the *Carmina Gadelica*,[2] the collection of religious songs and blessings gathered from the Highlands and Western Isles of Scotland by Alexander Carmichael (1832–1912), gave impetus to a tendency which has inspired the writing of many prayers and liturgical forms which are also described as 'Celtic'.[3] The precise sense in which these prayers are 'Celtic' is difficult to determine. The vicar of Lindisfarne, David Adam, is a notable contributor to this more recent development.[4] The

---

[2] The term 'Celtic' is so vague that it is sometimes of little use. What is meant by the term? We can define 'Celtic' in very precise terms as a particular people in a particular historical location. That is the predominant use in this book. There is also a more loose definition concerning themes such as the Celtic attention to scripture or its apparent affinity with nature. On occasion some have tended to use the term to describe contemporary poems and hymns composed by people who happen to live in Scotland, Ireland, Wales, or even Northumbria. Simply echoing a distant tradition cannot be an adequate meaning for the term 'Celtic'.

[3] It should also be noted that Carmichael was part of a group whose explicit concern was the continuation and recognition of the oral tradition of the Highlands. One may expect that Carmichael chose only the very best and most 'Celtic' of examples for his collection, and that those he chose may have been smoothed out in rhythm and content. We cannot therefore consider them typical of the Celtic tradition.

[4] David Adam has published many books along these lines, two of which are *Borderlands* (SPCK, 1991) and *The Rhythm of Life* (SPCK, 1996). It is important to remember that, perhaps more than drawing on a 'Celtic tradition', Adam is basing his poems and prayers on the tidal lifestyle involved in living on Holy Island and the weaving and mining imagery of the time and location in which he grew up.

implication for the unwary is that somehow the original liturgy
of the Celtic church has been recovered. This is simply not so.
There are some surviving Celtic prayers, blessings and liturgies
(such as the Stowe Missal) but again, these are not indications
of an original and single Celtic liturgy belonging to a single
Celtic church. Rather, they represent only the survival of a
number of local and particular traditions not necessarily uniquely Celtic so much as being Christian documents from a period of
time when the Celtic saints were active.

The process of romanticising the Celtic church has tended
to go far beyond an attempt merely to recover ancient forms of
prayer. It has tended to encourage a rather vague mysticism
which does not really seek to recreate an older Celtic tradition
so much as to press it into the service of what Meek calls a
'Celtic New Religious Movement'.[5] The core contention of
such a tendency is that the Celtic church is an older and more
authentic version of a Christianity that we have lost and that
needs now to be recovered. There are many versions of such a
feeling – because 'feeling' is what it is rather than an attempt
at genuine historical research.

The writings of Shirley Toulson represents one strand of
such an attempt. Her book *The Celtic Alternative: A Reminder
of the Christianity We Lost*[6] connects the Celtic church with a
number of modern movements ranging from Buddhism to the
Women's Movement, the Green Movement and the Peace
Movement.[7] Donald Meek lists some of the historical inaccu-
racies and inadequacies of such an approach. He rightly

---

[5] Meek, 'Modern Celtic Christianity', p. 9.
[6] (Rider, 1987).
[7] Ibid., pp. 13–15.

comments that the parts of the Celtic witness that are inconvenient in such an identification are simply ignored. He notes the attempt of one of the writers attached to the Little Gidding community to link creation spirituality with the Celtic church and asks, 'Is Little Gidding going in for a little kidding?'[8]

Meek's question is a fair one, not only in relation to the Toulson and Little Gidding end of the spectrum. His observation can also be fairly applied to a more broadly charismatic interest in the Celts as found in the writings of Ray Simpson, Michael Mitton and some of the New Church groups who seem to have discovered the Celts in recent years. Simpson, for example, considers the downfalls in the more 'typical' charismatic approach which he describes as 'importing flavour of the month spirituality', and how 'Charismatic renewal has no future unless it touches what is truest and deepest in our British Culture.'[9] Simpson speaks also of his experience of the influence of Celtic spirituality:

> Celtic Spirituality resonates with leaders of House Churches and other denominations. One House Church leader happened to hear some worship led by musicians of the Northumbria Community at a gathering for northern church leaders at Bradford Cathedral. Although he had no place for liturgy in his tradition, this Celtic-style worship reduced him to tears ... This man was always active, totally committed, a church planter. He read aloud some words pinned on to a book-end

[8] Meek, 'Modern Celtic Christianity', p. 17.
[9] Ray Simpson, *Exploring Celtic Spirituality* (Hodder & Stoughton, 1995), p. 19.

about there being a contemplative in all of us, and
he began to weep; a new dimension of God was overwhelming him.[10]

Finney speaks also of charismatic movements whose 'emphases
have a strongly Celtic flavour – it is more life-affirming and
more ready to accept the role of the imagination than either
traditional Catholicism or Protestantism; it believes in a God
who works in the everyday lives of people; it expects God to
act; it is prepared to experiment'.[11]

These words of caution do not suggest that we cannot usefully reflect on the spirituality of the Celtic church, but there
is a difference between seeing some of the resonance of the
Celts for our time and claiming that somehow the Celtic
church can be authentically recast to meet our present needs.
F. J. Saunders Davies writes of the relevance of Celtic spirituality for today by pointing to underlying themes in contemporary culture, the sense of being overwhelmed by the threat of
extinction, and the need to recreate a sense of human belonging and identity.[12] Using the Celts as resource in the quest for
spirituality is rather more legitimate than overromanticising
our connectivity with a hidden Celtic past.

---

[10] Ibid.
[11] John Finney, *Recovering the Past* (DLT, 1996), pp. 143–4.
[12] Unpublished article *Light in Darkness: The Relevance of Celtic Spirituality Today*. In this extensive article Saunders Davies starts from the contemporary position of a world under threat and uses that model to see how the tra-
ditions of Ireland, Scotland and Wales – themselves under some cultural
threat – can provide inspiration. Saunders Davies sees this pattern reflected
not only within the Celtic lands but also without, for example in the writings of theologians such as Moltmann.

RESCUING THE CELTS

This all suggests that if we are to make any useful sense of the Celtic church, we need to engage in something of a rescue exercise in order to see their significance more clearly. Such a rescue does need to take the historical record as seriously as possible. With that in mind, how then do we assess the Celtic church? Three responses to the Celts are common amongst writers.

The Failure of the Celts

To some extent this is the view of the victors. In simple form it argues that the Celts fade from the historical scene precisely because of the weaknesses of their position. The fact of their fading proves their failure. What do we make of such a judgement? To some extent the Synod of Whitby as told by Bede (part of the tradition of the victors) reinforces this view, as he found many aspects of the Celtic tradition attractive. Bede rightly recognised that he owed a debt to their work and had to admire their tough spirituality at a time when he felt the church was becoming rather too soft in its spiritual disciplines. But the picture he presents of the debate, and especially of the deciding role of the king, was that the Celts were no match for the intellectual rigour of the Romans, not able to benefit from the strength of a single continental authority, too divided and uncertain to contest the obvious advantages of Roman organisation and resource.

Even for those who were fond of them, such as Bede and the king, the Celts had to be seen as the past. For all with eyes to see, Rome represented the future. Perhaps there might even have been some sense of the parallel between the shift in secular power from the Romano-Celts to the new Angles and Saxons and what was now taking place in the ecclesiastical realm. This view of the Celts has had sufficient strength, an argument from apparent success, that it has dominated our understanding of the Celts for centuries. They were so ill-organised, on occasion irascible, and even worse – extreme in their views – that their fading was inevitable.

But is this a fair and accurate assessment? Two points need to be made. First, the Celts did not fade from the scene following Whitby. Indeed, their contribution in the British Isles and across Europe continued with some brilliance for centuries. Recent and continuing research is uncovering the astonishing extent to which this is true. Certainly the Celtic stream was gradually subsumed in terms of local ecclesial authority by the re-emergence of the parish and diocesan system and in monastic terms by a more uniform, and arguably simpler, Benedictine form. But that fading has as much to do with the invasion of the Norsemen and the disruption of the home base as it has to do with the inherent weaknesses of a distinctively Celtic contribution.

Second, no movement lasts forever. The fact that it does not is no indication of its relative worth. The record increasingly reveals that the Celts made a major contribution to the conversion of Europe, to the transmission of an older scholarship to a largely illiterate Europe, and to the spiritual discipline of Europe. That this outstanding contribution lasted for hundreds of years and was resourced primarily from the relatively small population of Ireland is hardly a failure so much as a glittering success story. Instead of asking why the Celts failed it might be more pertinent to ask what it was about their tradition that enabled such a contribution to be made from so slender a resource.

The Disaster of Whitby

A second distinct view, and one that is not necessarily recent, views Whitby as a disaster. Those who take such a view do not form a uniform group but there are a number of themes that emerge. For example, the victory of the Romans at Whitby is seen as the beginning of an unholy alliance between state and church in the same kind of way that the conversion of Constantine is seen by some as a disaster, not a victory. The implication is that the Whitby outcome was decided by the secular authority and not by the Christian community. It was therefore an imposed decision which brought the church under secular authority and virtually guaranteed the later descent into medieval corruption.

Such a tendency forms part of the 'what if' or 'if only' approach to history. If the Celtic party had won the debate at Whitby, wouldn't the history of the church in Europe have been markedly different? Such a view almost certainly attaches too much importance to Whitby and does not take account of broader developments in Europe as a whole. While a victory for the Celtic party at Whitby would have prevented the partial exodus of Irish monks from Lindisfarne it is unlikely that the eventual picture of the English church would have been any different from that of Ireland, Scotland and Europe as a whole. The major recruiting arm of the Celtic church remained that of Ireland, and the Irish church was well on the way to accepting the position of Rome on such matters as the tonsure, the date of Easter, and indeed all of the other matters debated so fervently at Whitby by the time that the Synod of Whitby was called.

Even so, it can still be argued that it would have been better if the Celtic church had maintained its influence within the totality of the European church. Apart from the fact that it is hard to imagine what series of events would have been necessary to have arrived at such an outcome, it becomes very difficult indeed to imagine what the eventual outcome might have been. It is possible that a number of regional centres of influence might have emerged to challenge the dominance of Rome, in much the same way that the Eastern church was able to maintain its regional distinctives based on Constantinople, Alexandria and Antioch. But although local traditions might have remained as more diverse than a single Roman pattern, the move towards a more uniform pattern of diocese at the expense of monastery, and accommodation between state and church as a precursor to the emergence of Christendom, may not have been much different in substance from that of a wider Roman pattern found in much of Western Europe.

The Value of the Celts

The observation that Christendom was likely to develop for other reasons leads fairly remorselessly to a consideration of another perspective which emphasises the contribution of the Celtic church, while recognising the apparent inevitability of a broader move towards a uniform pattern of ecclesial development relating strongly to Rome. John Finney, one exponent of such a view, suggests that the Celtic form of church was useful in the initial growth of the Christian mission, but that its pioneering work needed to be replaced by a more settled pattern of parish and diocese:

> When a large group of people are not Christian, living in a society which has attitudes and an ethos which are

not Christian, then the Celtic model of evangelisation is more effective ...

> After the 'conversion' of a nation or a community, when a 'Christendom' situation obtains, then a settled Roman pattern is more satisfactory ...

> Where there is a 'mixed economy' – where Christendom still has some vestiges of its former glory (and such communities still exist in many places) – we need a mix of both Roman and Celtic forms of ministry.[13]

In short, the Celts represented the early phase of mission, but it needed to be consolidated by something else. John Finney is an Anglican bishop and it is tempting to think that this is the kind of conclusion that you would expect an Anglican bishop to arrive at. But that would be unfair to Finney.

The strength of Finney's argument lies in the recognition that although there are differences in the approaches of the Celtic church and the Roman missions, there are also similarities. For example, although Boniface and Columbanus might have had difficulty in working with each other, and each saw the distinctives of their respective missions, the pagans amongst whom they were working might not have seen many differences, if any. In one sense, both the Celtic and the Roman missions had an early phase which did begin to change in approach as the context became increasingly dominated by a Christian consensus. Evangelism gave way to education.

But it is difficult to accept entirely what looks like a fairly cosy conclusion. Finney rightly points out that the Celtic

---

[13] Finney, *Recovering the Past*, p. 141.

model as we have come to know it was a mission model. But is it inevitably the case that mission should fade from the life of the church as the church becomes a dominant social and ecclesial reality? Might it not also be argued that the great weakness of a post-Celtic Christendom is that mission was excluded in favour of a rather inward-looking concern for the development of a Christian culture and society? Can the church really be the church without mission? Might the radical nature of the Celtic church have been helpful in acting as the cutting edge of a church that had forgotten mission and instead sought to defend temporal Christian boundaries? Would the crusades have taken place if a Celtic understanding of mission had remained at the heart of a European church? Would *peregrinatio* rather than crusade have brought an entirely different kind of relationship with Islam? These too can become 'what if' questions, but from the perspective of contemporary mission, rather than historical assessment, they might be questions worth asking.

THE FASCINATION OF THE CELTS

If we are asking these kinds of questions concerning the Celts then a different kind of assessment of their contribution might become possible. I want to suggest three ways of understanding the Celtic church as preparation for some reflection on what we might usefully learn from them in the contemporary scene. In this sense, learning from the Celts is different from a highly questionable attempt to mourn their passing or, even worse, to recreate the Celtic church.

First, the Celtic church represents one of the older forms of the church in Europe. It was not the only older form of the church in Europe but there is good reason for thinking that the shock of the arrival of large numbers of pagans in Europe dealt the existing local churches a severe blow. That would hardly be surprising. The whole of the existing European civilisation had been given enough of a shock that even Pope Gregory was inclined to think, not just that the end of civilisation had come, but that the end times themselves had arrived.[14] A largely urban society, and a largely urban church had been uprooted by new peoples who were tribal in nature, rural in their settlement patterns and pagan in religious practise. The existing Christian communities hardly knew how to respond, and in fact were initially largely unsuccessful in any missionary sense. That was why mission came mainly from two centres: from Rome, which had learnt how to contain the pagan threat, and from those parts of the British Isles which had not seen a pagan invasion but which had recently been converted from a pagan past.

The older and diverse Christian traditions of the continent looked to Rome for help and naturally accepted patterns from that source. The Celtic tradition preserved not one but a number of older local Christian traditions and it was this memory of an older tradition, for example the inspiration of Martin of Tours, that the various Celtic groups had preserved and developed in local forms. In their Celtic form these traditions had not had the experience of being overwhelmed by paganism. Rather, the opposite was true. They were shaped by the

---

[14] Pope Gregory considered the end of the world to be imminent. Although he observed what he believed to be the apocalyptic signs of Luke 21:25–33 all around him, Gregory saw the apocalypse coming not within his own lifetime, but soon after. For an account of Gregory's eschatology see R. Markus, *Gregory the Great and His World* (CUP, 1997), pp. 51–4.

experience of mission and demonstrated the radical confidence of such a church.

Second, the interface between the Celtic church and pagan religions is potentially instructive. This is not to suggest that lessons cannot also be learnt from the Roman approach. Both have their own importance and indeed it is unwise to draw too sharp a distinction between them as if they were almost different religions. But the understanding that the Celts had of the essentially tribal basis of the newer pagan peoples did contrast with the urban perspective of Rome. The Celtic missions never gave the same priority to establishing city bases for their ecclesial centres in the way that the Roman missions did.

It has sometimes been noted that the Celtic church had no martyrs. Some have attempted to draw the conclusion that this was because they accommodated pagan beliefs within their missionary approach. That contention seems highly improbable. Another possibility is that they understood their adversaries sufficiently well that they knew how to bring them to the gospel in ways that were powerfully winsome. We might usefully learn from the nature of this powerful winsomeness.

Third, the Celtic church was almost defined by mission as if mission were its very *raison d'être*. Those engaged in thousands of missionary journeys — some like Columbanus well known and well remembered, many utterly anonymous — were never emissaries in the way that the Roman missions sometimes seemed to be. The compulsion to engage in wanderings for Christ flowed from an awareness that the heavenly kingdom was almost more real than this world. They were not trying to establish a church order on earth so much as expressing the essential unity of the cosmos reflected by the coming of the High King of Heaven. Heaven was being brought to earth rather than the earth being accommodated to heaven. There was no reporting back to a single directing authority. Rather, the impulse for mission was contained within the very self-replicating nature of the communities themselves. Founded in mission, engaging in mission, they continued to train missionaries wherever they were.

It is this missionary character, the ability to contextualise mission, and their awareness of their own foundation in mission from which we can learn lessons for our present situation.

What then do we make of the Synod of Whitby and the supposed clash between a Celtic and a Saxon tradition? We must remember that we only have one account of that event: Bede's. It is very much the story as told by the newly dominant Saxon voice. The differences that were genuinely debated at Whitby were not critical in terms of a clash between a unified Celtic church and a unified Roman church. In fact, the churches in the various Celtic areas did not all practise the same thing. It could, however, be said to be a clash between a number of local traditions and a growing wider tradition. The general approach of Celtic missions was both to maintain local tradition and to some extent to resist a harmonising tendency. But the difference does not lie in a clash between liturgies, doctrine and organisation so much as in a culturally distinct approach to the task of mission.

The importance of the Celtic missionaries is that they understood the essentially tribal basis of Celtic society and of the newly arrived pagan Angles, Saxons, Franks, Goths, Vandals and Visigoths. The tribal similarities between the earlier pagan Celts and the new arrivals stood in stark contrast to the essentially urban Christianity associated with southern European Christianity. Indeed, part of the unique contribution of Martin of Tours was his concern to reach beyond the urban centre, where Christianity was well established, to the pagan hinterland, or country people, who had not been touched by the gospel. It is not surprising that, although he was not himself a Celt, he acted as an inspiration to the Celtic saints.

This ability of the Celts to contextualise the Christian faith in a mission to the tribes marks their significance for the Christian history of Europe and accounts in large measure for their astonishing achievements. This book is concerned with understanding those achievements and with describing the ingredients that made their mission so effective. Although we no longer live in a tribal society, and we must be cautious about drawing cosy romantic conclusions, there are some aspects of our present age into which the Celtic saints may speak.

12

COMING HOME:
LEARNING FROM THE CELTS

 The sense of 'coming home' felt by many in modern Western culture when encountering the Celts needs to be taken seriously.[1] There is an issue here that lies deeper than a mere desire to romanticise the past, although, as I have suggested, the risk of romanticising is ever present. Many have argued that Western culture is either in crisis, or dramatic change, or both. This crisis or change is sometimes referred to as a discontinuity with the immediate past and is sometimes characterised as a shift from modernity to post-modernity. Many writers have spoken of the radical despair that has questioned the earlier optimism of the experiment of the Enlightenment. David Harvey describes both the hopes of modernity and its ending in these words:

> Writers like Condorcet ... were possessed of the extravagant expectation that the arts and sciences would promote not only the control of natural forces but also understanding of the world and of the self, moral

---

[1] The theme of 'coming home' is discussed in the preface.

progress, the justice of institutions and even the happiness of human beings.

The twentieth century – with its death camps and death squads, its militarism and two world wars, its threat of nuclear annihilation and its experience of Hiroshima and Nagasaki – has certainly shattered this optimism. Worse still, the suspicion lurks that the Enlightenment project was doomed to turn against itself and transform the quest for human emancipation into a system of universal oppression in the name of human liberation.[2]

Anthony Thiselton outlines the 'principle of suspicion' that underlies much of the thought of postmodern philosophers, so that 'The postmodern self perceives itself as having lost control as active agent, and as having been transformed into a passive victim of competing groups. Everyone seems to be at the mercy of someone else's vested interests for power.'[3]

Nowhere is the suspicion of humankind's attempt to control its destiny felt more acutely than in humanity's interaction with the natural world. The sense that the Enlightenment's 'will to power' has brought the threat of annihilation rather than liberation is clearly demonstrated in the dramatic rise of ecological concern. As Ian Bradley has put it:

The battle to save the environment has captured the imaginations of millions of people, not just those who

---

[2] David Harvey, *The Condition of Postmodernity* (Blackwell, 1988), p. 13.
[3] Anthony Thiselton, *Interpreting God and the Postmodern Self* (T. & T. Clark, 1995), p. 12.

vote for the Greens or join Friends of the Earth. It is now firmly on the mainstream political and social agenda and can now no longer be dismissed as a fringe issue of interest only to cranks and faddists.[4]

These shifts in the concerns of many in Western culture are often deeply felt rather than fully understood, but they are nonetheless potent because of it. A feeling that religion is somehow more important than previously supposed, a search for wholeness as compared with an earlier scientific reductionism (which sought to explain the universe only in terms of its constituent parts), a suspicion of an unbridled technology (especially in its ecological impact), are all underlying – even if unarticulated – concerns. These feelings, which have caused so much space on the shelves of our booksellers to be taken up with books loosely in the area of Body, Mind and Spirit, represent potent signposts which help us to understand what lies behind the notion of 'coming home'.

THE MOUNTAIN BEHIND THE MOUNTAIN – A NEW CELTIC MISSION?

What is it that the 'stonehuggers' of Iona intuitively sense about the Celtic tradition that evokes the feeling of homecoming? Is it the case that a sense of alienation brought about by the crisis of modernity and the despair of postmodernity generates a search for an older wisdom? Is this merely an attempt to leapfrog over the immediate past of the Enlightenment to

---

[4] Ian Bradley, God Is Green (DLT, 1990), p. 1.

recover a continuity with an earlier age? What should the church in the West in its present missionary response learn from the ancient Celts?

The obvious lesson to draw is that there is much in the life of the Celts that naturally resonates with current concerns. Many of these themes have been explored in the earlier chapters of this book. The affirmation of women and the feminine, the embrace of the natural world, an identification with the poor, the inclusion of laity in the monastic life, and the positive place of the arts in community life. These and other themes are clearly attractive in a culture where the dominance of the male has been called into question, where hierarchy is rejected in favour of more open, or 'flat' structures, and where the arts are celebrated as offering signs of transcendence in contrast to the suspicion with which science is often viewed. But three words of caution are essential.

First, it is all too easy to read into the past what we want to see. While it is certainly true that women found a more prominent place in the Celtic communities than they did in the Roman missions, it would be just as foolish to interpret Celtic Christianity as a forerunner of the Women's Movement as to think of the Celtic saints as the first Western Buddhists.

Second, we must always remember that any description of the Celtic church will be selective to a greater or lesser degree. Books, such as this one, are open to the accusation that only the attractive (for this generation), and so convenient, aspects of Celtic Christianity are described. There are also some potentially unattractive aspects of Celtic practice that are seldom mentioned. Not the least of these was the tendency towards nepotism in the selection of successors to the powerful abbots of the best-known monasteries. These lines of successors could sometimes look like tribal dynasties.

Third, it is essential to avoid crass imitation. It is difficult to avoid the feeling that some are tempted to recreate a Celtic church by attempting a crude incorporation of the Celtic themes that seem the most attractive. We do not learn through a process of imitation nor can imitation ever be authentic.

But that does not mean there is nothing to learn and reflect upon. The problem is to know how to approach the matter. One writer who is himself a Celt with deep feelings of an imbibed tradition uses a fascinating concept in order to approach the Celtic mindset. He has used the phrase the 'mountain behind the mountain' as offering a way in to understand a broader Celtic tradition. He offers these words to describe what he means:

The mountain behind or within the mountain is not the perfect or ideal mountain in some Platonic sense. Neither is it that mythical Mount of Parnassus on which the Muses dwell. Nor yet is it the Holy Mountain in which God reveals himself in theophany or transfiguration. Each of these mountains belongs to its own mind-set, its own world of imagination. The mountain of that kind of Celtic tradition to which Kathleen Raine belongs, and which nurtured the people from which I came, is neither an ideal nor a mythical mountain, nor is it exactly a holy or sacred mountain in the sense of a mountain made sacred by theophany or transfiguration. No, it is a very ordinary, very physical, very material mountain, a place of sheep and kine, of peat, and of streams that one might fish in or bathe in on a summer's day. It is an elemental mountain, of earth and air and water and fire, of sun and moon and wind and rain. What makes it special for me and for the people from which I come is that it is a place of Presence and a place of presences. Only those who can perceive this in its ordinariness can encounter the mountain behind the mountain.[5]

In other words, the first mountain at which we look obscures a second reality. We actually have to climb the first mountain to see the hidden mountain. This second reality is not just an abstract idea that underlies the first concrete reality – it too is a physical reality. For example, Christians like to speak of the importance of fellowship. We might say that the first mountain is the regular coming together of Christians in worship services and in small groups. The hidden mountain is not therefore a mere mystical appreciation of the meaning of meeting. For Christians it has to be the reality of developing deep friendships in which forgiveness and mutual service is actually worked out. That would be a 'hidden mountain' in this Celtic sense.

In terms of a specific learning from the Celts, what then is the mountain behind the mountain which needs to be perceived? Five themes emerge as useful descriptors of this hidden mountain.

1. The New Monasticism

The trend towards radical individualism in the West, seen in the gradual decline, first of the extended family and now increasingly in the disintegration of the nuclear family, seen

---

[5] Noel Dermot O'Donoghue, *The Mountain Behind the Mountain* (T. & T. Clark, 1993), p. 30.

too in the wider weakening of community so that institutions as diverse as political parties, the trade unions, the Boy Scouts and the churches are increasingly unable to attract members, has produced a strong counter-desire for the experience of meaningful relationships. The late 1960s and early 1970s witnessed the growth of a wide range of attempts at community life, most of which ended in failure. What mattered was not so much the failure of particular experiments as what the various attempts signalled in terms of a core desire for the experience of authentic community. Many social commentators have described the growth of fundamentalism in all of the major religions, together with the rise of a variety of authoritarian cults as a reaction to the rise of individualism.

The mainstream churches have for the most part found it difficult to respond to the rise of individualism. The very notion of congregation, whether in the form of a parish or a gathered congregation has tended to perform a role in relation to a wider community. The collapse of a strong sense of belonging to a wider community – a village, a small town, a well-identified suburb – has produced its own problems for the church.

Generally speaking, churches have tended to respond in one of three ways. First, some congregations want to promote a sense of community in the wider neighbourhood, both through the activities of the church in a direct sense and through offering the facilities of the church to groups with a community emphasis. Some churches have been successful in this attempt, but it is almost certainly a minority that have a major impact in the promotion of a wider sense of community, at least in a Western European context. Those who attend such churches might have a sense of well-being in that the community is well represented in the broader life of such a congregation, but intimate fellowship is often absent.

Second, there are those congregations which attempt a broadly consumerist approach in that they see the needs of individuals and attempt to meet them. Those needs might be approached by targeting particular groups within the community – youth, men, young families and so on – or by offering the kind of attractive worship services where felt needs are met through the worship style and the subject matter of the sermon. The programmes that such a church offers are usually good and those who attend might well feel that the obvious needs of their family are well met. Indeed, they may even have good relationships with others in their peer group. But what may be missing is a specific commitment to the development of deeper relationships.

Third, some congregations attempt to act as alternative communities. Although this can sound like a sect or even a cult, it does not have to be so. Some congregations, particularly in urban settings, have been able to create such communities, although they do tend to be small in size. The feeling in such a church is that group loyalty is the paramount consideration. The encouragement of a deeper journey within, or even the asking of questions which might disturb the group, are not always welcome. It will be obvious that these three approaches are not necessarily mutually exclusive and some congregations may see themselves as evidencing a mixture of these approaches.

While no-one would wish to belittle any of the above approaches, and although it can be argued that some congregations display a lively and vigorous community life, it is difficult to see such communities providing the sense of 'homecoming' of which we have been speaking. There is a deeper ache for the kind of relationships by which we can understand not only others but also our own being.

What some have called the 'new monasticism' offers one way in which the need for belonging can be addressed. In recent years, a number of communities and orders have begun to practise forms of monastic life that can be open to others who are outside the immediate community.[6]

In common with the earlier Celtic monasteries the rules of these various communities are somewhat diverse, but three characteristics seem to feature widely. These are the principle of accountability, availability, and participation in the regular prayers. Each of these principles can be expressed in a wide variety of ways in different traditions, but there are obvious similarities with an older monasticism. What makes this a 'new' monasticism is the fact that both men and women, lay and ordained, can participate in a meaningful community as a fairly disparate network. The 'mother' house provides the sense of physical home, while the disciplines of accountability, availability and prayer provide an emotional and spiritual home.

This is not to say that this kind of life cannot happen in the local church and is restricted to monastic communities. Indeed, one senses that the best use of monastic community is to act as a kind of 'experimental hothouse' to discover precisely what 'community' might mean so that local churches can be helped to foster that kind of community experience. I have met Christians who have described to me their local church in just such terms. However, we do need to be realistic and

---

[6] The best-known communities in a British context are Iona and Northumbria. Iona has some 220 members and 1,600 associates, most of whom do not live on Iona. The author Ray Simpson has a useful survey of communities in his book *Exploring Celtic Spirituality* (Hodder & Stoughton, 1995), especially pp. 7–14.

acknowledge that such powerful experiences of the local church are currently the exception in the Western world.

2. Spirituality

The idea of spirituality can be a very diffuse notion. What does it mean in the context of the mountain behind the mountain? In one sense spirituality can mean anything and everything that cannot be contained by that which we call the material. Even a table might have an element of spirituality attached to it if the designer saw in it a thing of beauty around which people would meet to share in discussion, in work or in eating together. But the meaning that I want to give spirituality relates more to the very practical understanding which it has come to assume within a specifically Christian tradition. Here we can think of three closely related elements.

First there is the God encounter. Those who speak of a God encounter do so in a wide variety of ways. It might be a profound consciousness of the presence of God received in meditative silence or in exuberant praise. The experiences of each individual in this matter can be extremely diverse. There is no single way in which God is made manifest in the lives of those who seek him. What matters is not the circumstances of the encounter so much as the encounter itself. It is an experience of the other, the holy, of a transcendent reality which allows individuals to see themselves from the perspective of another centre, and so in a completely new light. The God encounter is not a matter of mere feelings, a time of warmth and personal comfort. In profound form it produces the conviction of the saints that at the end of all things, all will be well. This is not merely a matter of sentiment, but flows from an awareness that the ultimate reality, the ground of being, is that the one who is all and stands behind all, is love.

Second, there is the journey within. To know and experience God allows us also to explore much that is within our own lives. Some writers describe it as an exploration of the shadow side of who we are. The shadow side exists at many levels. It can mean those parts of our being that we prefer not to acknowledge and which in our naïvety we believe we can hide from God and ourselves. Indeed, there is the constant fear that if we acknowledge the shadow side of our being God will then find us out and somehow find us unacceptable.

The shadow side can also be those parts of our being that are the reverse of the stronger parts of our personality that have remained unexplored during the first part of our life. For example, someone who is naturally very extrovert may never have explored silence and meditation. The second part of our life offers an opportunity to open up the slightly less dominant streams of our personality. Journeying within needs to be undertaken in the context of the God experience. To be assured that we stand in the love of God gives us the confidence to tenderly explore the areas where we might normally feel unsure and even unsafe. The experience of the cell, where one is alone for long periods of time, offers a context and a discipline in which one can be found by God and find oneself. The ending of activity is a necessary discipline to journey within.

Third, there is compassion for others. It is no accident that when disasters occur and the camera crews arrive with the world's press, Christians are often already on the ground acting to alleviate suffering. Nor is it a coincidence that many orders of monks and nuns are associated with care for the poor and the hurting. Christian spirituality is never complete without a deep interaction with the world. Withdrawal to the cell is for the purpose of a more creative engagement with the world. Many have realised that solitude is actually essential for solidarity with the world. As Kenneth Leech expresses it: 'Solitude plays a vital part in helping us to be disentangled, focused and committed. It is not surprising that today more and more committed people are being attracted by the image of the desert and solitude.'[7]

The interaction between the God encounter, the journey within and the engagement with others in a spirit of service means that Christian spirituality is immensely practical. It is therefore a very tangible 'mountain' behind the mountain.

3. Liturgy

We have already described the 'new monasticism' and that carries with it an implication that liturgy is part of the landscape. That is indeed true, but it is not a matter of including liturgy simply because it is part of monastic life. Strictly speaking it does not have to be so. It is possible to imagine a solitary life in which a liturgical life was not present. Yet, significantly, even those who live as hermits find that they do require a liturgy of sorts to sustain the life of prayer.

Of course, there is nothing magical or even necessarily mystical about the forms and words of liturgy itself. There is an inevitable tendency for the beauty of a liturgy to become frozen in time so that it loses its original accessibility. The opposite danger is that the words and forms are so immediately relevant that they become banal.

---

[7] Kenneth Leech, *The Sky Is Red*, (DLT, 1997), p. 37.

Good liturgy should remind the worshipper of the natural rhythms of life. The times of prayer within a 24-hour cycle, the weekly celebration of communion and the seasonal festivals all point to the fact that we exist as creatures bound by time. Paradoxically, good liturgy celebrates our place as 'time bound' beings precisely in order to point to the eternal, to the one who is not bound by time. It is a means of connecting a material world with a reality that transcends and includes it. According to Kenneth Leech: 'The history of Christian liturgy is the history of offering material things to God.'[8]

The rediscovery of liturgy as a centre point for life is essential. Such recovery produces a place where music, art, architecture, colour, dance and drama can combine to celebrate the meaning and purpose that God brings to our lives. What matters is not the first mountain, the art and music by itself, but rather the second mountain which seeks to weave all these elements into a tangible, participative, liturgical drama.

4. Sacrament

For very obvious reasons, sacrament and liturgy are intimately connected. The eucharistic drama forms the heart of the major liturgical act in the Christian community. At its very centre the Christian community, whether it be a monastic community or a local church, must be a eucharistic community. The celebration of the drama of the Lord's supper not only connects the church with the first disciples and with the message of the cross, but with ancient Israel too.

---

[8] Ibid., p. 168.

But the sacraments are not limited to communion. Here I do not mean to number the sacraments at all. It matters little in the sense in which we are now speaking whether we say that there are two sacraments or five. As with the Orthodox, the mountain behind the mountain declares that the sacraments cannot be numbered since all of life is sacred.

The Celts had a fundamentally sacramental theology. We should not imagine that their embrace of nature meant that they were really the first 'Greens'. That is to miss the point entirely. Nature was hardly under threat because of the axes of the Saxons in the same way that it is as a consequence of modern insecticides. The ecological agenda is inevitably a modern phenomenon. Nor is there any suggestion that the animism of some who are neopagans in the Green movement is essentially sacral in their view of creation. As an earlier chapter maintained, for Christians the world is good because the Creator is good, not just because the natural world sustains us. It is not therefore a matter of imitating modern pagans in their regard for the created order. It is much more a case of bringing a proper balance or holism to our view of the world by means of a sacramental view of faith and mission.

And here we probably do need to make a choice. It is difficult to see how the theology of crisis that underlies much talk of revival can be reconciled with a sacramental approach to life. A sacramental theology is always world affirming, seeing the creation as essentially good. Crisis theology has a fatal tendency towards a world-denying view of life.

Here lies a curious paradox. It was precisely the world-affirming desert fathers who gave up all creature comforts in favour of a life of prayer, while those with a crisis theology tend to denounce the world, and seem so comfortable with a gospel of health and wealth. What is at stake here is a sacramental view of life that sees the creation as sufficiently good that it must be treasured, valued and properly approached in order that it may be enjoyed. Abstinence and fasting is a means of appreciating the value of food and not just a way of avoiding unhelpful excess.

If there is to be a crisis in the lives of those to whom we take the gospel, it should not be simply a moment of personal spiritual or psychological crisis. The gospel seeks to induce a much deeper crisis as authentic sacramental communities act out a counter-culture which challenges the deeper values of a world in disarray. There is to be a power encounter as the true God challenges the idolatrous images of consumerism and individualism. The god of the market place must fall just as surely as did the pagan gods of the pagan Saxons.

We are called once more to infuse the secular with the sacred because it is only from the perspective of the sacred that the secular can be truly good and so truly be enjoyed as God intended. Such a view is not merely a naïve return to a world without cars and phosphates. It is not merely a re-enchantment with nature. A Christian view of nature recognises that evil is also present in the created order and has not solely been introduced by the industrial revolution. Nature as much as humanity waits and groans for redemption. The 'red in tooth and claw' theme in nature is still a reality. (As one humorous farmer suggested on a roadside sign: 'Try British lamb, 50,000 foxes can't be wrong'!) A sacramental view of the world recognises the evil as well as the essential good that underlies creation and attempts to bring the love of the Creator to bear in all things. The development of communities that act out a counter-culture of love and care represent the mountain behind the mountain.

5. Movement of the Imagination

As we reflect on the astonishing missionary movement gener-
ated by the Celtic saints, the sheer numbers of missionaries
involved strikes home again and again. Although it was not
always young people who responded, they often did. Somehow
the Celtic movement managed to capture the imagination of
generations of young people on a huge scale. It is not enough
to talk of strategies, or methodologies. That is only to see the
first mountain. The real mountain that released the energy of
this movement lay in a movement of the imagination.

That movement is not merely the creation of communities, although it results in that, nor is it produced entirely by
the creative leadership of outstanding individuals, though that
also took place. In the first instance the movement of the
imagination was fired through an encounter with a new biblical agenda. That is why the Celts found scripture to be so
important. The biblical narrative introduced them to a new
world of hope. The kingdom of God, which they sought to
declare and demonstrate, acted as 'the core metaphor for a new
social imagination'.[9] It was this new metaphor that was prayed
for and preached about.

Crucially, that new metaphor, or horizon of hope, offered
individuals a key place in the accomplishment of such a dream.
Here lay one of the main differences between the Celtic communities and the Roman monasteries. In the Roman tradition
the community itself offered the mentoring or training of the
noviciates. The vision was one of becoming part, usually a very

---

[9] Quoted by Leech from Walter Brueggemann, *Hope within History* (John
Knox Press, 1987), p. 22.

small part, of a greater whole, a larger civilisation, which had its roots in Rome. Given the struggles of the land, there was a certain safety and attraction in such a life.

The Celts offered a different vision. The only greater whole for them lay beyond the grave. They sought to bring the light of Christ to bear on that which they met. They were mentored in the process, directly by their soul friends and therefore indirectly by greater men in the monastery. The goal was that one day they would be one of these wanderers for Christ, making a unique contribution according to their call. It was this passion that allowed the young to respond and the mature to be able to live alone, perhaps in a Swiss valley, gradually bringing a whole tribe, a set of farms and villages, to know the overwhelming power of God and the light of Christ.

The challenge to make a difference and the ability to offer a context in which that difference can be realised is one of the critical issues facing the church in the West at this time. It is clearly not enough to offer challenges that are not based on any ability to make a difference. Faced with the overwhelming pressures of our present culture it might be tempting to despair and so to abandon any prospect of offering any challenges to anyone. But if history teaches us anything, it is that movements begin on the fringes of society. Small numbers of innovators can make huge differences both for good and for ill. Tomorrow belongs with those whose imaginations can seize it and whose commitment wills it.

GLOSSARY

MAIN PEOPLE, PLACES AND PHRASES

Adamnan: In 679 Adamnan was chosen as abbot of Iona, where he then, around 680, proceeded to write the biography of St Columba. The annals suggest that Adamnan was around the age of fifty-two when he wrote Columba's *Life*, so we can assume that Adamnan was born around the year 627. After spending some time in both Northumbria and Ireland, during his abbacy of Iona, Adamnan died in 704.

Aidan: Originally based in Iona, Aidan, in response to a call from Oswald, left to preach to the Anglians of Northumberland. He spent much of his life at the monastery on Lindisfarne ministering to many noblemen and holy men. Aidan died on 31 August 651.

Anamchara: The Irish word for 'soul friend', the person many holy people took as confidant and personal judge of spiritual matters.

Armorica: The old word used for the area on the most westerly peninsula of Gaul known more commonly as Brittany. Many Britons from Cornwall, Devon and Wales are thought to have migrated to this area as a direct result of Irish immigration into those areas.

Athanasius: Athanasius is important not so much because of what he did, but for what we can learn from him about the early Christians in Britain and the heritage that they adopted. The most significant aspect of this heritage is probably that of desert asceticism, for the activities of the desert fathers may well have been communicated to Gaul through him while he was in exile from his Alexandrian bishopric in Trier in 336.

Augustine: Augustine was sent from Rome by Pope Gregory in order to preach to the British. Augustine arrived in Kent in 597 and was given permission to preach by King Ethelbert. Augustine sought out representatives of the Celtic churches in order to encourage catholic unity, but he ultimately failed. He died on 26 May 604.

Bede: Bede, born around the year 673, wrote one of the main primary sources for the story of the Celtic church in Britain, namely his *History of the English Church and People* (731).

Bobbio: Location in northern Italy of a monastery, with its famous library, founded by Columbanus.

Brehons: Lawyers within Irish society.

Brendan: Brendan came from County Kerry. He grew to know Comgall with whom he travelled to Iona, where he became a friend and disciple of Columba. His intervention at the Synod of Meltown in Meath had the excommunication of Columba rescinded. In his seventies he went to Galway where he founded Clonfert, before returning to his sister in Annaghdown where he died in the year 578 at the reported age of ninety-two.

Brigid (Bridget, Bride): Brigid was born in County Louth around 450 and died in 523. She was the supposed first woman priest who founded a mixed monastery at Kildare.

Brude, King: Received the gospel from Columba and his party from Iona.

Cadoc: Welsh saint who founded, amongst others, the monastery Nant Carfan, west of Cardiff.

Candida Casa ('the white house'): The centre of St Ninian in Galloway modelled on the monastery founded by St Martin at Tours.

Carmichael, Alexander: Compiled the *Carmina Gadelica*, a nineteenth-century collection of Highland prayers and blessings finding inspiration in the lives of the Celtic saints and their preoccupation with work and nature.

Cassian, John: Responsible for establishing a community near Marseilles and author of *De Institutis Coenobiorum* and the *Collationes*.

Columba: Born in 532, Columba studied under Finnian and Mobhi and by the aged Gemman. Founded his first monastery in Derry in 546. In 561 he feuded with King Dermot of Ireland. Abbot of Iona from 563–597.

With Comgall and Kenneth, visited Brude and converted the Picts. His missionary disciples were Machar of Aberdeenshire, Cormac of the Orkneys and Moulag of the Western Isles. He died in 597.

Columbanus: Born around 543, Columbanus schooled at Sinell's and Comgall's. Columbanus travelled to France, attacking the church for simony and observing Easter at a different time. He exhorted Boniface IV to be more careful in conduct. Retiring to the Apennines, between Genda and Milan, he built a monastery at Bobbio which was consequently much visited by other saints and holy people. He died in 615.

Comgall: Disciple of Fintan of Cluain-Edrech and teacher of Columbanus, Comgall founded Ireland's greatest church at Bangor. He visited Columba on Iona and journeyed with him through the Great Glen to preach to the Pictish King Brude. Comgall died around the year 602.

Cuthbert: Schooled at Melrose Abbey by Eata, Cuthbert became a disciple of Aidan and later located at Lindisfarne. He was made a bishop at the Synod of Twyford and consecrated by Theodore. In 685 he was consecrated bishop of Lindisfarne where he died in 687.

Dal Riata (Dalraida): Originally referring to a small Irish kingdom in the north of Antrim, Dal Riata became more commonly used within a Scottish context, and was spoken of in terms of a dynasty up to the twelfth century.

David (Dewi Sant): David's birth, prophesied some thirty years before, took place in the year 462. He went on to establish the monastery of Menevia in Glyn Rosyn. A leader of the Welsh church, he established the Synod of Llanddewi Brefi and Synodud Victoriae in Caerton. David had many holy friends and family ties. He refuted the Pelagian heresy. David died in 547.

Druids: Priestly class within the pre-Christian Celtic lands.

Eata: Disciple of Aidan, he was the first Abbot of Melrose where he taught Cuthbert. He became the Bishop of Hexham after the Synod of Whitby in 678. He was Bishop of Lindisfarne in 681 for three years.

Edwin, King: King of Northumberland, converted by Paulinus in York in 627.

Ethelberg: Queen and wife of Edwin who took Paulinus as her chaplain.

Finbarr: Early Irish missionary said to have taught Columba. Legend has it that Finbarr crossed the Irish Sea on horseback in order to preach to those in Argyll.

Finnian of Clonard: Cadoc brought Finnian to Wales in order to study. He went on to teach both Columba and Columbanus. He died from the plague in 549.

Finnian of Moville: Finnian of Moville was also connected with Columba, but was his pupil. Finnian also spent some time studying in the famous Candida Casa.

Eriugena, John Scotus: Born around the year 800, this Irish theologian based at Laon and Rheims produced work that reflected the Greek classics, especially Neoplatonism. Eriugena was a significant member of the court of Charles the Bald and stands as a direct bridge between the scholasticism of the Celts and the traditions of Greece and even Syria. He died around 877.

Galloway: Eventual settling place of St Ninian, in southern Scotland.

Gaul: The old Roman word for France.

Germanus of Man: Worked with Patrick in Ireland and lived afterwards in a monastery founded by Illtud. In 466 he was ordained Bishop of the Isle of Man.

Gildas: Born in the Clydesdale region of southern Scotland around 516, Gildas went on to study under Illtud. Welsh monastic leader and author of several works including the *History and Epistle*. He died around 570.

Gregory, Pope: Sent Augustine to Canterbury to work with the English.

Hilda: Baptised in 628, as a young woman she heard Paulinus preach and was taught by Aidan at Lindisfarne. She was the Abbess of Hartlepool after Columbus. In 657 she founded her own double monastery. She worked with Cuthbert to reconcile differing doctrines between the Roman Catholic and Celtic wings of the church.

Honoratus: Fifth-century founder of the monastery at Lerins, a group of islands off the coast of Provence. His monastery became a famed centre of learning and several bishops studied there.

Illtud: Born in Armorica around 450, Illtud spent his early life as a soldier and husband before becoming a monk. He founded a monastery at Llantwit Major and taught many great holy men. Illtud died in 535.

Iona: Holy island off the shores of Mull in Western Scotland where Columba founded a spiritual community after leaving his native Ireland.

Julius: Little-known figure whom Gildas refers to as a martyr of the early Christian church in Britain.

Kenneth: Educated by Finnian and Cadoc. Friends of Columba, they undertook missions together and later settled on the island north of Iona. Kenneth was also founder of Agaboe.

Kentigern (Mungo): Reared by Serf at Culross, he settled in Glasgow with missionary ventures to Strathclyde. Fleeing to Wales, he was welcomed by David and founded a monastery at Llanelwy, returning to Scotland around 573. He died around 612.

La Tene: Period in early, pre-Christian Celtic lands, defined by a particular artistic style.

Liber ex Lege Moisi: A form of a Celtic book of law.

Lindisfarne (Holy Island): Island off the coast of Northumbria where Aidan established a monastic centre.

Literati: Strata in Irish society below noblemen including brehons, druids and bards.

Martin: Bishop of Tours, 316–97. He trained under Hillary and led the Gallacian church, derived from the East rather than Rome. He influenced Ninian in particular and a whole host of others with his brand of asceticism. He died in Candes on 11 November 397.

Ninian (Bynia, Nynia, Ringan, Nenn): After studying in Rome, he was ordained a bishop. Returning from Rome, he met Martin at Tours who influenced him in his building of Candida Casa in Galloway. Converting the eastern Picts, he went as far as Orkney, Shetland and the Great Glen, founding many churches and chapels along the way. He died in 432.

Oswald, King: King of Northumbria whose wanderings in exile had taken him to Iona. It was Oswald's appeal that brought Aidan to Northumbria and Lindisfarne. Oswald died in a battle at Maserfield in 641.

Palladius: First bishop to the Scots (the Irish), ordained in 431, he was a forerunner of Patrick. Sent by the Bishop of Rome (Celestine) to convert the Irish. His mission was short-lived and ineffective.

Patrick: Born in 389, Patrick was snatched as a boy and sold into slavery in Ireland for six years where he tended sheep before his escape. Patrick returned to Ireland at forty years of age to evangelise, and won over the druids. He established contact with the church of Palladius and baptised King Laoghaire's daughters, thus bringing the monarchy to Christianity. Patrick died in 462.

'St Patrick's Breastplate': Patrick's famous prayer of protection.

Paulinus: Sent in 601 by Pope Gregory to assist Augustine in his work with the English. Paulinus became Bishop of York.

Pelagius: Probably an Irish monk, Pelagius' life is one of uncertainty. He entered into bitter wranglings with Augustine over the nature of grace and human free will.

Peregrinatio pro Christo: The self-imposed life-pilgrimage for Christ undertaken by Celtic saints.

Picts: Originally one large kingdom in northern Scotland, the Picts were, by the time of Bede, divided into the northern and southern Picts. The southern Picts were said to have been converted first by Ninian, and the northern later by Columba. There is much discussion as to the politics of the region the Picts inhabited, both between themselves and external parties such as the Romans.

Poitiers: Location of probably the first monastic centre in the West founded by St Martin of Tours around 360.

Saining: Practice undertaken to insure that no evil spirits are present.

Samson: Taught as a child by Illtud at Llantwit Major. He established his own monastery on Caldey Island. Samson died in 565.

Sedulius Scotus: Irish scholar of the ninth century who had a large impact on the court of Charles the Bald.

The Senchus Mor: The law of the Brehons established with the assistance of Patrick.

Serf: Disciple of Palladius and Ninian, he nurtured the infant Kentigern. Evangelist of Fife, he went on to establish a monastery at Culross.

King Sigibert: King of the East Saxons who, in 604, was converted by Augustine.

Stowe Missal: Example of a Latin liturgy native to Celtic regions.

Teilo: A relative of David, he succeeded Dyfrog as Bishop of Llandoff. Famous for making a pilgrimage to Jerusalem.

Tours: Location of St Martin's second monastery founded in 372 which went on to be a model for Ninian's Candida Casa in Galloway.

Whitby: Location of the famous Synod debating the date of Easter in 644.

SELECT BIBLIOGRAPHY

Adam, D., *Tides and Seasons* (Triangle, 1989)

Allchin, A., *God's Presence Makes the World: The Celtic Vision through the Centuries in Wales* (DLT, 1997)

Bamford, C., and Marsh, W. (eds.), *Celtic Christianity: Ecology and Holiness* (Floris Books, 1982)

Bede, *A History of the English Church and People* (Penguin, 1988)

—, *The Life of St Cuthbert*, in *The Age of Bede*, trans. J.F. Webb, ed. D.H. Farmer (Penguin, 1965)

Berresford Ellis, P., *Celt and Saxon: The Struggle for Britain* (Constable, 1993)

Bitel, L., *Isle of the Saints* (Cornell University Press, 1990)

Bowen, E., *Saints, Seaways and Settlements* (University of Wales Press, 1977)

Bradley, I., *The Celtic Way* (DLT, 1993)

—, *God Is Green* (DLT, 1990)

—, *Columba: Pilgrim and Penitent* (Wild Goose Publications, 1996)

Browne, G.F., *The Christian Church in These Islands before the Coming of Augustine* (SPCK, 1899)

Carmichael, A., *The Sun Dances* (Floris Classics, 1988)

Chadwick, N., *Studies in the Early Christian Church* (CUP, 1958)

—, *The Age of the Saints in the Early Christian Church* (OUP, 1961)

Chadwick, N., *The Celts* (Penguin, 1971)

Davies, O., and Bowie, F., *Celtic Christian Spirituality* (SPCK, 1995)

De Paor, L., *St. Patrick's World* (Four Courts Press, 1993)

De Waal, E., *The Celtic Vision* (DLT, 1988)

—, *A World Made Whole* (Fount, 1989)

Dillon, M., and Chadwick, N., *The Celtic Realms* (Weidenfeld & Nicolson, 1967)

Dodd, B., and Heritage, T., *The Early Christians in Britain* (Longmans, 1966)

Donaldson, C., *Martin of Tours: The Shaping of Celtic Spirituality* (Routledge, 1997)

Doyle, P., *The Latin Bible in Ireland: Its Origins and Growth in Biblical Studies: The Medieval Irish Contribution* (Dominican Publications, 1976)

Drane, J., *Evangelism for a New Age* (Marshall Pickering, 1994)

Duncan, A., *The Elements of Celtic Christianity* (Element, 1992)

Finlay, I., *Columba* (Chambers, 1992)

Finney, J., *Recovering the Past* (DLT, 1996)

Forrester, D., *The True Church and Morality* (WCC Publications, 1997)

Foster, J., *They Converted Our Ancestors* (SCM Press, 1965)

Gallyon, M., *The Early Church in Northumbria* (Terence Dalton, 1977)

Godel, W., 'Irish Prayer in the Early Middle Ages', in *Milltown Studies*, vol. 9 (1982)

Gougaud, L., *Christianity in Celtic Lands* (Four Courts Press, 1992)

Green, M., *The Gods of the Celts* (Alan Salton, 1986)

Hanna, J., *The History of the Celtic Church* (Edward Brothers, 1962)

Hanna, W.A., *Celtic Migration* (Pretina Press, 1985)

Hardinge, L., *The Celtic Church in Britain* (SPCK, 1972)

Harvey, D., *The Condition of Postmodernity* (Blackwell, 1988)

Henken, E., *Traditions of the Welsh Saints* (D.S. Brewer, 1987)

Herbert, M., and O'Riain, P. (eds.), *Betha Adamnain: The Irish Life of Adamnan* (Irish Texts Society, 1988)

Herbert, M., *Iona, Kells and Derry* (Four Courts Press, 1996)

Hughes, K., *Church and Society in Ireland, AD 400–1200* (Variorum Reprints, 1987)

—, *Early Christian Ireland: Introduction to the Sources* (Hodder & Stoughton, 1972)

John, C., *The Saints of Cornwall* (Lodenek Truran, 1981)

Kelly, J., *The Hiberno-Latin Study of the Gospel of Luke in Biblical Studies: The Medieval Irish Contribution* (Dominican Publications, 1976)

Knox, R., 'John Scotus Eriugena: An Irish Biblical Scholar', in *Irish Biblical Studies*, vol. 7 (1985)

Laing, L., *Celtic Britain* (Routledge & Kegan Paul, 1979)

Lehane, B., *Early Celtic Christianity* (Constable, 1994)

Lines, M., *Sacred Stones, Sacred Places* (Saint Andrew Press, 1992)

Low, M., *Celtic Christianity and Nature* (Edinburgh University Press, 1996)

MacNeill, E., *Celtic Ireland* (Academy Press, 1981)

McDonlad, S., *The Greening of the Church* (Geoffrey Chapman, 1990)

McNamara, M., 'Celtic Christianity, Creation and Apocalypse, Christ and Antichrist', in *Milltown Studies*, vol. 23 (1989)

Meyer, K., *Ancient Irish Poetry* (Constable, 1911)

Mheara, R., *In Search of Irish Saints: The Peregrinatio pro Christo* (Four Courts Press, 1994)

Mitton, M., *Restoring the Woven Cord* (DLT, 1995)

Moran, D., *The Philosophy of John Scotus Eriugena* (CUP, 1989)

Mould, D., *The Celtic Saints* (Clonmore & Reynolds, 1956)

Murphy, G., *Early Irish Lyrics* (Clarendon Press, 1956)

O'Laoghaire, D., 'The Eucharist in Irish Spirituality' in *Doctrine and Life* vol. 32, p. 595 1982)

—, 'Some Comments on "Irish Prayer In the Early Middle Ages" by W. Godel', in *Milltown Studies*, vol. 10 (1982)

O'Donoghue, N., *The Mountain Behind the Mountain* (T. & T. Clark, 1993)

O'Dwyer, P., *Celi De: Spiritual Reform In Ireland* (Carmelite Publications, 1977)

—, *Towards a History of Irish Spirituality* (The Columba Press, 1995)

O'Meara, J., *Eriugena* (Clarendon Press, 1988)

Peterson, E., *The Message of Scotland's Stones* (P.C.D. Ruthven Books, 1996)

Rees, B., *Pelagius: A Reluctant Heretic* (The Boydell Press, 1988)

Ross, A., *The Pagan Celts* (B.T. Batsford, 1986)

Ryan, J., *Irish Monasticism* (Irish University Press, 1931)

Sellner, E., *Wisdom of the Celtic Saints* (Ave Maria Press, 1993)

Sharpe, R., Adamnan of Iona, *Life of St Columba* (Penguin, 1995)

Sheldrake, P., *Living Between Worlds* (DLT, 1995)

Simpson, R., *Exploring Celtic Spirituality* (Hodder & Stoughton, 1995)

Spence, H., *The Church of England, a History* (Cassell, 1897)

Thiselton, A., *Interpreting God and the Postmodern Self* (T. & T. Clark, 1995)

Thomas, P., *Candle in the Darkness* (Gomer, 1993)

Toulson, S., *The Celtic Alternative: A Reminder of the Christianity We Lost* (Rider, 1987)

—, *The Celtic Year* (Element, 1993)

Wessels, A., *Europe: Was it Ever Really Christian?* (SCM Press, 1994)

Whiteside, L., *In Search of Columba* (The Columba Press, 1997)

Also available from HarperCollins*Publishers*:

Anglo-Saxon Christianity

Paul Cavill

Celtic spirituality was not the only form of early Christianity in the British Isles. In fact, a larger number of original texts from the Anglo-Saxons remain today. This rich vein of simple, but moving, prose and poetry is explored in *Anglo-Saxon Christianity*. The key figures of Bede, Cuthbert and others are introduced alongside new translations of classic texts taken from Beowulf and Old English poetry.

For all who appreciate Celtic spirituality, here is a fresh and alternative source of nourishment and inspiration. For those looking for an authentic Christian faith *Anglo-Saxon Christianity* reaches back into the very birth of the English people.

Dr Paul Cavill is a former UCCF staff worker and now lectures in Old English at the University of Nottingham, England.

Christian Books

Timeless truths in shifting times

www.christian-publishing.com

News from a Christian perspective

Exclusive author interviews

Read extracts from the latest books

Share thoughts and faith

Complete list of signing events

Full catalogue & ordering

www.christian-publishing.com